COLLINS GEM
ANTIQUE MARKS

a mine of information

COLLINS GEM
D

CH00726498

COLLINS GEM
CRICKET

a mine of information

COLLINS GEM
DIETING

a mine of information

COLLINS GEM
DOGS

a mine of information

COLLINS GEM
FIRST AID

a mine of information

COLLINS GEM
INTERNET

a mine of information

COLLINS GEM
PREDICTING

a mine of information

COLLINS GEM
Ready
REFERENCE

a mine of information

COLLINS GEM
SHARKS

a mine of information

COLLINS GEM
WHALES & DOLPHINS

a mine of information

COLLINS GEM
WHISKY

a mine of information

COLLINS GEM
WORD PROCESSING

a mine of information

COLLINS GEM
Your PC

a mine of information

COLLINS GEM

FASHION

Joshua Sims

HarperCollins*Publishers*

The right of Joshua Sims to be identified as the author of this
work has been asserted by him in accordance with the
Copyright, Designs and Patents Act 1988

HarperCollins*Publishers*
Westerhill Road, Bishopbriggs, Glasgow G64 2QT

First published 2000

Reprint 10 9 8 7 6 5 4 3 2 1 0

© Essential Books 2000

Pictures by kind permission of: John Adrian, Camera Press/
Leon Herschtritt/Deborah Hood/Relang, Friends of the
V&A/Daniel McGrath/Sara Hodges, Chris Moore, Pictorial
Press, The Press Association, Rex Features

ISBN 0 00 472476-3

Printed in Italy by Amadeus S.p.A.

Contents

Bibliography

The Fashion Book
(Phaidon, 1998)
Fashion, A Concise History
(Gertrud Lehnert,
Laurence King, 1999)
*Fashion and Fashion
Designers*
(Georgina O'Hara Callan,
Thames and Hudson,
1998)
Kenzo
(Ginette Sainderichin,
Thames and Hudson,
1999)
Shoes
(Linda O'Keefe,
Konemann, 1996)

Introduction

Whether it's the New Chic or Street Glamour, Retro Boho or Sport Luxe, fashion can now incorporate any personality, lifestyle, fantasy or fetish. It's elitist and populist, it revolutionizes our thinking and plunders the past and it's as seductive and fickle as sunshine. From the catwalks of haute couture to the chain stores on the high street, we are all involved, whether we choose to be or not. In the Western world it impossible to purchase even the most basic items of clothing without adding to the fashion honey pot. The plainest of jumpers will have been modulated according to this season's colours and cut. As fashion expands its source bank further and further (looking to other cultures for inspiration, incorporating sports clothes and utility wear into its market) even the most hermetic of consumers cannot avoid its influence.

Our lives become more and more styled, with even the choice of cutlery and car upholstery requiring a tricky design decision, and we have developed an ever more discerning eye for our image and the differing statements clothes can make. We can't avoid choosing what we wear (we have to wear something, after all) and as we are encouraged to develop our own individuality in a third millennium which offers so many routes to self-discovery, we are acutely aware that our clothing is the most effective way to make a statement about ourselves.

Whilst the range of looks from which we can make our choice broadened during the twentieth century, and high style no longer means one particular style, fashion has perhaps become less radical. Imagine the early eighteenth-century dresses of the French court, or the ruffs, slit fabrics and stockings of sixteenth-century male fashion, and we see that high fashion has become less exclusive, more eclectic and more wearable, but also less extreme. The present is a less revolutionary period than we like to think.

However, at the elite end of fashion, in the arenas of high concept and haute couture design, the outrageous persists, from Gaultier's 1991 conical breasts to Galliano's 2000, down-and-out inspired deconstruction of the art of tailoring.

Both frivolous and essential, fashion inspires and gives flesh to every personal fantasy. In those parts of the world fortunate enough to have money to spend on more than essentials, fashion filters further through the population than any other art form. Creatively, the world's top designers shape the zeitgeist, and economically, as an international industry supporting thousands, it is a business world of considerable power.

The World of Fashion

The seeds of the fashion industry as we now know it, and indeed the culture of label-orientated consumerism, were sown with the genesis of haute couture. Both the creative zenith of fashion and the pinnacle of exquisite craftsmanship, haute couture was first recognized and organized with the formation of the Chambre Syndicale de la Confection et de la Couture Parisienne in 1868.

With the growth of the bourgeoisie came the need for advisers in matters of style. The creation of the Chambre, a response to the need to regulate the expanding number of couturiers and to protect their work from plagiarism, marked the shift from individual styling to prescribed styling. Creative control of a woman's appearance passed out of her and her seamstress's hands and into those of the predominantly male couturier. It was now he and not the wearer who coordinated the shape of a dress, the choice and purchase of the fabric, the selection of buttons and bows, gloves and hats. This was the origin of the label and, in many ways, of the male shaping of the female ideal.

Over the years the Chambre has become part of the Fédération Française de la Couture du Prêt-à-Porter des Couturiers et des Créateurs du Mode, an umbrella organization for designers of ready-to-wear (prêt-à-porter) clothes as well as couture houses. Its rules currently require a couture house to employ at least twenty people in the workshops and show at least fifty new pieces to the fashion press in Paris twice a year. In 1946, 106 workshops were registered as couture houses: by 1997 there were only 18.

Constructing couture items remains an intricate and traditional process, with each piece made to measure. Every garment is the result of expensive and labour-intensive workshop hours from an army of seamstresses, button makers, jewellery designers, hat makers and embroiderers. Before World War II there were perhaps as many as 40,000 couture clients, but now the figure is nearer 2000. As expensive as a work by a prominent painter, with a small cocktail dress perhaps costing £15,000, the increasingly exclusive world of haute couture is important for public relations and the development of new ideas, but is no longer financially lucrative.

The haute couture Paris shows in January (for the spring/summer seasons) and in July (for autumn/winter) are now fantastic extravaganzas. Unconstrained by cost or practicality, designers have the chance to make art out of clothes and display them in lavish, stage-managed sensual experiences, where music, lighting and performances elevate the events from fashion shows to fashion theatre. Whilst the London, New York and Milan fashion weeks major in prêt-à-porter, the escalating emphasis given to the overall show experience is clear there too. The pressure to show, to be seen by the world's press, is resisted by few designers.

The high cost of couture gave rise to the prêt-à-porter label, where a designer's signature style, the combination of tailoring and styling that gives each their recognizable look, can be acquired more affordably, in off-the-peg outlets. Equally the growing exposure and influence of fashion houses encouraged them to develop 'diffusion lines', either alternatively named labels targeting a different market, maybe a younger or sportier one, or ranges of accessories, from perfume to golfwear and sunglasses, to complement their branding.

As with all industries, the fashion world is driven by its most successful engines – the major fashion labels. Some are couture houses with ready-to-wear lines and some are purely prêt-à-porter. The fortunes of these companies can be

broken or revived by the success and stature of their main
designers. Karl Lagerfeld has been employed by major, long-
established couture houses such as Chanel and younger
houses such as Chloé, but has also continued to show and
sell under his own name. Fashion incorporates rebels too:
Givenchy appointed the radical young designer Alexander
McQueen. The new and the old need and feed off each
other within the industry in the same way that fashion itself
continues to feed off its past – just as Vivienne Westwood,
the grande dame of high-concept fashion, plunders the
romance of the past in her trademark bustles and bustiers.

Using the Gem Guide to Fashion

This introductory guide to the world of fashion takes the
major labels, the most important names in fashion, as its
starting point. Entries begin with the founders of the often
eponymous labels, and their date of birth. Major designers
who have shown and achieved recognition with their own
labels are to be found under their own names, even if they
currently design for a long-standing house. Entries cover a
wide range, and have been chosen for their importance.
Biba, for example, was a shop rather than a haute-couture
house, but the label was seminal in shaping the style of the
1960s. Biographical details of founders and designers are
given (this is an industry driven by personalities and tastes
more than any other), and business developments and
transactions are included to provide a broad picture of the
fashion world and the financial powers driving it.

Azzedine Alaïa

Founder: Azzedine Alaïa
Born: 1940, Tunisia

Azzedine Alaïa's style is a deceptively simple one. His structural clothes are intricately constructed, each garment hand-finished and tailored in such a way that it cocoons the body. He refers to himself as a *bâtissuer*: an architect, a builder of clothes, rather than a fashion designer. In exploiting the principles of corsetry – using whalebones, stays and décolletage – he creates an undeniably flattering and feminine hourglass shape, one that made him a favourite of 1980s supermodels. This shape is reminiscent of late nineteenth- and early twentieth-century women's dress, and was revived in Christian Dior's post-war New Look. Perhaps unsurprisingly, Alaïa's clothes are not cheap.

The designer's signature style is a distinctive one. He uses knit fabrics extensively and favours punched and riveted leather, studded muslin, second-skin Lycra and wool, and inventive use of industrial zips on sexy dresses. Alaïa also successfully mixes fabrics in a way that other designers would balk at: tweed and silk jersey, glove leather and lace. He is always widening his use of fabrics, too, including 'houpette', a stretch fabric, and 'relax', a carbon-based anti-stress fabric used by NASA in floor coverings to repel electromagnetic waves. Alaïa does not conform to seasonal trends either. While other designers are all showing short skirts, his might be long or knee-length, and he has a reputation for showing extremely late each season – yet buyers and press seem content to follow his whims.

Indeed, Alaïa's contrary approach would, one might imagine, have gained him quick notoriety in the fashion world, but he has actually been designing for over thirty years. He studied sculpture at the Ecole des Beaux-Arts in Tunis, moving to Paris in 1957. He won an apprenticeship at Christian Dior – a prestigious position by anyone's standards – and left five days later. Alaïa spent just two seasons at Guy Laroche and a short time with Thierry Mugler, but built up his own private clientele, gaining discreet clients such as Greta Garbo, Cecile de Rothschild and Claudette Colbert, and launched his official first collection in 1981.

In Alaïa's spring/summer collection of 1992, his flattering, hand-finished tailoring was shown to its best advantage with the black hourglass dress

Giorgio Armani

Founder: Giorgio Armani
Born: 1934, Piacenza, Italy

Undeniably one of the most important fashion designers of the twentieth century, Giorgio Armani took his time to enter the fashion world. Born some fifty miles south of Italy's fashion capital Milan, he attended medical school at Milan University for two years, tried his hand at photography, completed national service in the army in 1957, and then worked at the department store La Rinascente as a window dresser. In 1961 Armani entered the fashion world proper, joining textile manufacturer and designer Nino Cerruti as a designer, where he stayed for nine years. Then, in 1970, with the assistance and encouragement of close friend Sergio Galeotti, he went freelance and designed for manufacturers such as Boulevard, Sicons, Montedoro and Gibo. He set up his own menswear label in 1974, destined to become a world leader in menswear design.

The following year Armani's menswear was ingeniously adapted to create a womenswear line, launched in partnership with Galeotti. It was an immediate hit: timeless, relaxed, unstructured, with exaggerated proportions and yet understated, a perfect selection of fabrics (wool, leather, suede, alpaca), precisely tailored and yet loose-fitting – and widely regarded as the most influential look since Dior's New Look (1947) and Quant's mini-skirt.

Armani's signature style was 1980s power-dressing,

Giorgio

snapped up by women finding themselves newly elevated to executive levels. By the late 1980s this wide-shouldered look was followed by a more slimmed-down version, still in Armani's favoured muted shades. The master of refined good taste – Armani is the polar opposite of Gianni Versace's glamour and glitz – the designer followed his daywear designs with eveningwear that would come to dominate Oscar night. Indeed, Armani's close relationship with Hollywood has always given him positive publicity, from dressing Richard Gere in *American Gigolo* (1980) to Diane Keaton in *Annie Hall* (1977).

However, this is not to diminish his enduring influence, nor his talents as a famous workaholic and clever businessman (despite a conviction for corruption in May 1996, along with designers such as Gianfranco Ferré). One of the first global household names to come out of the fashion world, Armani perfected the art of lifestyle branding, providing a modern, elegant but glamorous style for living through thirteen diffusion lines that have brought Armani style to an even broader market, from golfwear, jeans and fragrances to the lower-priced Emporio Armani.

By 1999, Armani's trademark 'power suits' of the 1980s had been replaced by more relaxed outlines, although muted shades were still used

Balenciaga

Founder: Cristobal Balenciaga
Born: 1895, Guetaria, near San Sebastian, Spain
Died: 1972, Javea, Spain

For most of the time that the legendary Basque tailor Cristobal Balenciaga was alive, his design house was at the heart of haute couture, with a status that verged on the legendary. Balenciaga trained as a tailor from the age of twelve, and was able to copy couture effectively by fourteen. He opened his own dressmaking/tailoring business in 1916, and moved to Paris in 1937 when the Spanish Civil War broke out. His distinctive pure lines and relaxed shapes ignored trends. His instantly recognizable pieces included flamenco-style dresses, jackets with big buttons and stand-away collars or three-quarter length sleeves, the controversial sack dresses of 1956 (later made popular by Christian Dior) and the pill-box hats first worn by America's first lady Jackie Kennedy in the early 1960s. Although essentially working from a sombre palette, by the 1950s he had also gained a reputation as a colourist, introducing pieces in bright yellow and pink.

Balenciaga worked to his own agenda, ignoring trends. When the mini-skirt arrived in 1966, he lowered hems, later creating a distinctive hem raised at the front and dropping at the back, and he cared little for the praise or criticism of other members of the fashion community. He refused to join the ruling body of Parisian fashion, the Chambre Syndicale

Modern Balenciaga design by Nicholas Ghesquière, combining transparent sleeves with the more traditional roll-neck (spring/summer 1999)

de la Couture, unlike his competitors Coco Chanel and Christian Dior. From 1957, he showed his collection, along with Hubert de Givenchy, at least a month later than other designers. However, Balenciaga was ready to quit in 1948 and continued only at the frantic behest of Dior. Designers André Courrèges and Emanuel Ungaro were among those who trained under him.

It has only been in recent years that the Balenciaga name has really begun to flourish again, largely due to the company's switch from couture to ready-to-wear in 1987. In 1986 the company was bought by the cosmetics group Jacques Bogart, who brought in designer Michel Goma, followed by Dutch designer Melchior Thimister in 1992. Under the young French designer Nicholas Ghesquière, appointed from within the company in 1997 against expectations of a higher-profile appointment, Balenciaga is now at the cutting edge of the industry. Recently, Balenciaga has been worn by Madonna and Sinead O'Connor, with pieces appearing in street- and youth-orientated fashion magazines. Many of Ghesquière's designs have stayed true to the Balenciaga feel: he likes to play with volume, for instance, giving jackets a fitted front and a voluminous back, or showing a skirt that reveals its composition of four separate panels when the wearer moves. Other provocative pieces from the young designer include bright white 'mentonnières', or wraps that go over the head and under the chin, structurally clean and true to Balenciaga, yet also reminiscent of hospital bandaging.

Voluminous three-quarter-length sleeves on a gown-inspired top by Ghesquière for the Balenciaga label (spring/summer 1999)

Pierre Balmain

Founder: Pierre Balmain
Born: 1914, St Jean de Maurienne, Savoie, France
Died: 1982, Paris, France

Forever associated with the internationally rich and leisured, Pierre Balmain designed essentially classic clothes for the over-forties. His womenswear is defined by its flattering simplicity and over the years he has gained many loyal fans, choosing elegance over more radical fashion, confident that these classic clothes will stand the test of time and trends.

However, although the Balmain look has remained consistent, business has not. Despite continued expansion in America, and the appointment of designers such as Oscar de la Renta, the house of Balmain dropped in value by 500 million French francs during the 1990s.

Balmain's father was the owner of a large drapery and textile business, so Pierre Balmain arrived in Paris already well-connected, with introductions to Jeanne Lanvin, Robert Piguet (Paul Poiret's assistant) and the English designer Captain Molyneux, with whom he began his apprenticeship in 1934. He originally studied architecture at the Ecole des Beaux-Arts in Paris, but failed to complete the course. In 1939, Balmain moved to Lucien Lelong with another young hopeful called Christian Dior, working so closely with him that their designs were distinctly similar.

Balmain launched his own fashion house in 1945. There

he created styles dominated by a long, slender sihouette, wide at the shoulders and tight at the waist, loose coats and the 'pantajudo', an intriguing hybrid of capri pant and skirt. The collection was immediately dubbed the New French Look by Balmain's friend Gertrude Stein. One style, a bell-shaped skirt, went on to become a big hit in Dior's New Look of 1947. From 1952, Balmain's collections centred on sportswear, suits and skirts with signature elements of flower-embroidered satin, high-waisted gowns and velvet cocktail dresses, all with hemlines resolutely below the knee. During the 1950s he created a trend for capes, as well as 1930s-style long-sleeved, ankle-length, figure-hugging sheath dresses that were worn under jackets.

Green cocktail dress from Balmain (autumn/winter 1998). For over fifty years the house has produced the ultimate in long, slender, elegant-silhouetted evening dresses

Biba

Designer: Barbara Hulanicki
Born: 1936, Palestine

Hulanicki and her Polish parents moved to London in 1948, with Hulanicki attending Brighton Art College before winning a beachwear design competition in 1955. She did not complete her course, but instead joined a company of commercial artists in London, drawing fashion illustrations for magazines and papers. She and Stephen Fitz-Simon married in 1961, and started a skirt mail-order company in 1963. It was the successful response to a pink gingham dress advertised in 1964 that encouraged them to open the first Biba shop that year.

The store sold Hulanicki's own designs, essentially that season's high fashion but at accessible prices. Attracting a dedicated type of young customer almost immediately – drawn to the store's mini-skirts, sweetheart-neckline T-shirts, and 1920s-inspired crepe dresses, smocks, trouser suits, mob caps and the floppy felt hats with which the Biba name became associated – two more shops were opened soon afterwards. Her clothes continued to be more fluid than many of the Mod-inspired geometrical designs of the time. The 1920s influence was also reflected in the three stores'

Twiggy in Biba's 'Rainbow Room' store, circa 1973. The combination of long satin dress, skull cap and gloves conveys the Art Deco influence in Hulanicki's designs

Art Deco interiors. They drew customers from all over the world, becoming tourist spots and focal points for the decade's buoyant fashion scene.

Biba kept trading until the early 1970s, taking over a department store in Kensington, London. The brand did not translate successfully into 1970s style, but on the strength of a 1960s revival, the Biba name was brought back in the mid-1990s with the opening of a store in London's Covent Garden that sold copies of Hulanicki's original designs.

Manolo Blahnik

Founder: Manolo Blahnik
Born: 1943, Santa Cruz, Canary Islands

Manolo Blahnik is arguably the most famous and influential footwear designer of his generation.

Born to a Czech father and Spanish mother, Blahnik studied law and literature at the University of Geneva before moving to Paris to study art at the Ecole du Louvre. He was working as a young set designer, dabbling with shoe design through the 1970s, when fashion editor Diana Vreeland saw his portfolio and encouraged him to start designing women's shoes full-time.

It was not long before the self-taught shoe designer had a well-established business on his hands. Blahnik moved to London in 1971, opened his first shop there in 1973, and became a key figure in the booming Glam scene

He quickly developed a clear signature style –

Blahnik evening shoes in floral brocaded silk, produced in 1996, show why 'Blahniks' remain the shoes of choice for celebrities the world over a witty and whimsical opulence in coloured leather, slippers, pumps and mules in kidskin, rich velvet or jewel-studded brocade, all with Blahnik's 'trademark' tapered vamp – and, before turning to dressier, more upmarket styles, designed the famous 'jellies' sandals for Elio Fiorucci. His sister, Evangeline, has worked with him since 1982, developing the business and the star-studded client list

Central to Blahnik's design approach is use of historical references. He borrows extensively from shoe designs of other eras, whether Regency or rococo, to create some of the most visually arresting shoes around, all hand-finished in his factory in Parabiago, Italy. However, his shoes are equally likely to draw on the more obscure corners of the twentieth century – such as one autumn/winter 1999 teal and gold sandal derived from the Bluebell Girls chorus line – or technologies of the present and near-future. One design from the same collection was described by the designer as 'aerodynamic, like the back of Concorde'. Art, such as work by Miró and Arp, is also likely to influence a Manolo design.

In the 1990s Blahnik taught design at the Royal College of Art in London. He has designed shoes for Ossie Clark, Calvin Klein, Yves Saint Laurent and Jean Muir among others, and his shoes have been used in catwalk collections by designers as diverse as Todd Oldham and Isaac Mizrahi.

Blahnik

Blahnik
and model

Bill Blass

Founder: Bill Blass
Born: 1922, Fort Wayne, Indiana, U.S.A.

A stylist as much as a designer, Bill Blass's skill has always
been in taking traditional garments and making them more
relaxed and wearable, softening the lines to create an
exaggeratedly feminine silhouette. He is also unique in his
combining of texture and pattern, adding innovative detail
to his renowned eveningwear, for example, by mixing smart
jackets mixed with gathered flounces at the hems of skirts.

Blass studied at the Parsons School of Design in New
York, joining sportswear manufacturer David Crystal in
1940 as a sketcher, before being drafted into the army in
1941. After World War II, he joined Anna Miller & Co as a
designer. The company merged with Maurice Rentner in
1950, with Blass moving up the corporate ladder to become
vice president in 1962. Eight years later, he bought the
company and renamed it Bill Blass. His first big hit came in
1963 with his best-selling summer dress with small ruffs at
the neck and hem. A dress with ruffed collar and cuffs was
worn by the quintessential 1960s model Jean Shrimpton in
an advertisement a few years later and created such demand
that it had to be put into mass production. Blass went on to
make a similar stir in 1966 with his white mink pea-jacket.

Blass style circa 1995. From the 1960s the label has been causing
a stir with its ruffed collars, cuffs, sleeves and hemlines

Bill Blass

Pierre Cardin

Founder: Pierre Cardin
Born: 1922, San Biagio di Callalta, Italy

Often overlooked and regarded as more businessman than designer, Pierre Cardin's creative talents have been eclipsed by his ability to put his name to just about any product around, from perfumes to ties (over 600 products by 1970). His skill at licensing his name is only matched by his ability to publicize it. Cardin's appearance on the cover of *Time* magazine had him clad in just a bath towel – a Pierre Cardin bath towel. By the same token, Cardin was the first French designer to establish markets in Japan (in 1958), China (in 1978) and more recently Russia. It was this business talent that made him not only a household name but also, at one time, the world's richest haute couture designer.

Pierre Cardin grew up in the Loire region of France, leaving home in 1935 to work for Manby, a tailor in Vichy. He moved to Paris after France's liberation in 1944, with the intention of studying architecture, but soon began working for Elsa Schiaparelli and the house of Paquin.

In 1946 he became head of Christian Dior's design studio. He set up his own business in 1949, making an odd mix of sober suits and extravagant theatre costumes (he had already designed costumes for Jean Cocteau's film *La Belle et la Bête* in 1947). In 1954 Cardin opened his first shop, called Eve, on rue du Faubourg Saint-Honoré in Paris, and in 1957 he launched his first womenswear collection. Ready-to-wear followed in 1963.

Cardin's widely influential, bold designs have always shown a taste for the future and the conceptual. Although associated with the use of knitted bodystocking-style fabrics, leggings and catsuits, in the 1950s he also designed bubble skirts, bias-cutting over a stiffened frame and unstructured shirts. He moved on to cut-out dresses (those with large sections removed from the sides or front) and outsized appliqué pockets in the early 1960s. Along with André Courrèges' collection of the same year, Cardin's 'Space Age' collection in 1964 comprised catsuits, batwing jumpsuits and helmets.

Perhaps Cardin's most distinctive contribution to fashion was his participation in the 'Space Age Style' movement which began in 1964. This example dates from 1967

Castelbajac

Founder: Jean-Charles de Castelbajac
Born: 1950, Casablanca, Morocco

Much of Jean-Charles de Castelbajac's work is primary-
colour bright and fresh from the playground, such as the
celebrated coat made from 39 teddy bears stitched together,
and he makes extensive use of logos, images and messages
drawn from cinema, advertising, art and any other field in
which he happens to be interested. Such pieces have led his
work to be tagged with the 'wearable art' label. De
Castelbajac does not stop at fashion: he has designed shoes,
jewellery and furniture, and art-directed *Faim de Siècle*, a
monthly newspaper that raises money for the homeless.

De Castelbajac entered fashion in 1968, through
designing dresses for his mother's clothing business,
Ko and Co. Before long he was designing for the
manufacturer Pierre d'Alby in Paris, where he was assistant
to Ziga Pianco. De Castelbajac presented his first show in
1970, gaining a reputation for turning household fabrics
such as blankets and gauze into clothes, and five years later
launched his own business – ironically gaining a reputation
for clean, modernist clothing that employed all the latest
hi-tech cutting techniques together with traditional fabrics,
such as his widely copied long quilted coat.

Hussein Chalayan

Founder: Hussein Chalayan
Born: 1970, Nicosia, Cyprus

Hussein Chalayan is one of only a few designers whose clothes are both concept-driven (i.e., originating from an idea or desire which extends beyond purely pleasing the eye) and wearable – although one of his less practical and more avant-garde creations was a bondage outfit without sleeves or armholes.

Chalayan graduated from London's Central Saint Martins College of Art and Design in 1993. Immediately he sold his graduate collection to Browns Focus, a small store specializing in cutting-edge designs. Such was the interest in his talent that he was quickly offered contracts with knitwear brand TSE and British high-street chain Top Shop.

He has stated his interest in the way clothes define what we are and the way we behave. His softly tailored clothes include representations of mathematics in beads on the matt jersey evening dresses that have become his signature style, and structural quirks, such as a shift dress with a back panel that billows away from the body. He also challenges the ethos of fashion and accepted ideas of beauty. In his autumn/winter 1998 show, the models wore bright red sticking plasters over their mouths and wooden cones on their heads.

Chalayan's quirky, cutting-edge designs challenge conventional fashion. In 1999 his shift dresses contained a panel altering not only the outline of the model but the way she moved

Chanel

Founder: Coco Chanel
Born: 1883, Saumur, France
Died: 1971, Paris, France

Coco Chanel always said that she designed only for
herself – to escape the flouncy and restrictive womenswear
of the early part of the century – and if anybody else
wanted to wear her clothes, that was up to them.

Coco Chanel's background was as unexpected as her
attitude. She was brought up in a convent, having been
orphaned at a young age. With every intention of becoming
a dancehall artist – her signature song was 'Qui qu'a vu
Coco?', hence the nickname – she entered the jet-set of the
time, thanks to the money and contacts of Etienne Balsan, a
Parisian playboy. Although details are scant, she is believed
to have picked up some dressmaking and millinery
experience along the way, and opened her first shop (a hat
shop) on rue Cambon in Paris in 1910. Further shops
followed in Deauville and Biarritz in 1915. World War I did
nothing to stop her customers from spending.

Buoyed by the shifting social scene of women in the
1920s, Chanel's simple, almost minimalist style grew in
popularity. Women could not get enough of her adaptations
of traditional menswear in an easy palette of black and navy
blue (as well as beige). Chanel offered light garments with
few linings, jersey dresses (first in 1916, when jersey was
generally used for underwear), sleeveless evening gowns,

loose blouses, 'yachting pants' – wide-legged sailor-style
trousers when trousers were still relatively radical – twinsets, beach pyjamas, straight skirts worn with Chanel's take
on a man's sweater, and the now staple Little Black Dress.

By 1921 Chanel had launched her first perfume – Chanel
No.5. During her time designing, Chanel was responsible for
putting gilt buttons on blazers, and introduced gilt-chained
handbags, strings of pearls (prefiguring her love of
extravagant costume jewellery in the 1970s) and slingback
sandals. She also designed clothes for Hollywood stars, most
notably Gloria Swanson.

While the company continued in a somewhat low-key
way, launching the quilted leather handbag and back-to-
back 'C' Chanel logo in 1955, Chanel herself all but
disappeared from fashion for 25 years. In 1954, at the age of
71, she came out of retirement and reopened her Paris shop,
surprising many with pre-war styles. This time she also
offered a less clean-cut look, including what has come to be
regarded as a quintessential Chanel garment: the jersey or
tweed, collarless, braid-trimmed suit with patch pockets and
knee-length skirt.

A similar slide into obscurity followed Chanel's death –
alone in the Paris Ritz – until designer Karl Lagerfeld took
over the house of Chanel in 1983. He cleverly dusted the
cobwebs off some of Chanel's older, now classic creations,
updating others (the hugely popular Chanel suit as black
leather biker gear, for instance) and generally reinvigorated
one of the biggest names in French fashion.

Chanel in 1992, post-Lagerfeld. The simple black, figure-hugging dress (worn, for added sophistication, with sunglasses and elbow-length gloves) was one of the most classic of garments to be given new life after 1983

Ossie Clark

Founder: Ossie Clark
Born: 1942, Liverpool, England
Died: 1996, London, England

Ossie Clark was the fashion darling of London's Swinging Sixties, and his work is still influential today. He studied at the Manchester College of Art from 1957 to 1961, then at London's Royal College of Art until 1964. His design work began with Quorum, a Chelsea shop that became one of the centres of the decade's fashion boom.

Clark joined Quorum as a full-time designer in 1966, producing gypsy dresses, hot pants and maxi coats – styles now regarded as quintessentially Sixties. He draped and scrunched fabrics such as satin and crepe (many designed by his wife Celia Birtwell) to make body-enhancing dresses and blouses with loose sleeves, nipped-in waists and revealing necklines, though one of his most widely-copied designs was a cropped leather biker's jacket with a large collar. In contrast to this 1960s sexiness, his 1970s work centred on an ankle-length dress, almost Edwardian except for leaving a flirtatious patch of bare skin on the lower back.

Clark still designed on a contract basis in the 1970s for a mass-manufacturer, but most of his later work was for private clients. He died in 1996 at the hand of his boyfriend.

Printed rayon, crepe and chiffon dress of 1969. Clark was particularly interested in the drape of fabric

Comme des Garçons

Founder: Rei Kawakubo
Born: 1942, Tokyo, Japan

Ask any architect, product designer or artist – not to mention any young fashion designer – who their favourite fashion designer is, or who has been their greatest influence, and there is a strong chance that the answer will be Comme des Garçons. The Japanese label, designed by Rei Kawakubo, has thrown away the rule book of cutting and construction and skirted the art world with clothes that challenge convention and invite more cerebral consideration than most. In 1987, just six years after her launch in fashion, the Fashion Institute of Technology named Kawakubo as one of the leading women in design this century.

Kawakubo began by reading literature at Tokyo's Keio University, but graduated in 1964 to join the Ashai Kasei textiles company. In 1967 she left to start her own business as a freelance designer, launching Comme des Garçons in 1969. Comme's menswear line was introduced in 1978 and fragrances have followed.

Since her first international collection, shown in Paris in 1981, Kawakubo's conceptual, androgynous designs have been hugely influential, often appearing in a more diluted form in other designers' collections. Her first collection introduced black, which until then was not the definitive

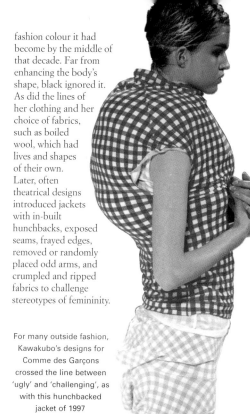

fashion colour it had become by the middle of that decade. Far from enhancing the body's shape, black ignored it. As did the lines of her clothing and her choice of fabrics, such as boiled wool, which had lives and shapes of their own. Later, often theatrical designs introduced jackets with in-built hunchbacks, exposed seams, frayed edges, removed or randomly placed odd arms, and crumpled and ripped fabrics to challenge stereotypes of femininity.

For many outside fashion, Kawakubo's designs for Comme des Garçons crossed the line between 'ugly' and 'challenging', as with this hunchbacked jacket of 1997

André Courrèges

Founder: André Courrèges
Born: 1923, Pau, France

Considered by many to be the father of futuristic fashion, André Courrèges created a minor revolution in fashion sensibility in the early 1960s: sharp, edgy, functional, austere clothes that are still influential today. Courrèges' key designs included mini-skirts, dresses with trousers, suits in silver, trapeze dresses (hung loose and parallel from the shoulder to the knee), white, square-toed leather boots ending at an unusual mid-calf length, sleeveless jackets and those with a cutaway, bodice-style fronts, hipster, bias-cut and tubular trousers, and goggles and odd helmet-shaped hats. The look was like nothing before.

Indeed, the bright white, super-clean 1964 collection which defined the Courrèges look was called the 'Space Age'. Courrèges subsequently introduced less exacting, more curvaceous styles, with bright colour trims to soften the impact of the harsh white, though futuristic cut-out dresses and Barbarella-style catsuits remained.

Courrèges first studied to become a civil engineer, but gave this up to work in fashion in Paris, joining Balenciaga in 1949. Courrèges remained with Balenciaga until he launched his own line in 1961, selling the business just four years later to L'Oréal. The styles he created were widely imitated, albeit often in more accessible, less threatening versions. Courrèges continues to design to this day.

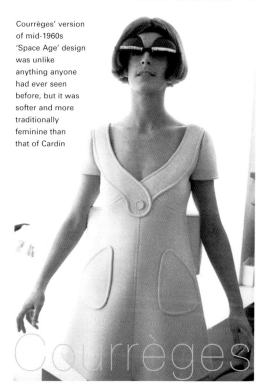

Courrèges' version of mid-1960s 'Space Age' design was unlike anything anyone had ever seen before, but it was softer and more traditionally feminine than that of Cardin

Christian Dior

Founder: Christian Dior
Born: 1905, Granville, Normandy, France
Died: 1957, Montecatini, Italy

Christian Dior's first steps into fashion were borne of tragedy. When he was 26 years old, in 1931, his father's business went bankrupt, his mother died of cancer and Dior contracted tuberculosis, which forced him to close the art gallery he had opened with a friend. Dior always insisted, most publicly in his autobiography, *Christian Dior and I* (1957), that his success was down to luck. He was reluctant to concede that his first collection – 1947's New Look – completely revamped women's fashion, moving it on from the restraints of war-time and emphasizing the sensuality of the female form for the first time in a decade.

After his family tragedies, a friend of Dior took to fostering his design talents by submitting his work to contacts in the fashion industry. By 1938, Dior had been hired by Robert Piquet's fashion house, only to find on his return from short service during World War II that the position had been given to someone else. Dior found work in 1942 at Lucien Lelong with Pierre Balmain. He then met Marcel Boussac, head of struggling fashion house Philippe

By 1997, the house of Dior was combining its tradition of beautiful tailoring with 'funky' design. The result was received with great excitement at the autumn/winter shows

and Gaston. Boussac asked Dior to help get the house back on its feet. Dior suggested that they open their own fashion house using his name and Boussac's financial and business backing. In 1946, the House of Dior was launched.

The New Look came to be regarded as quintessentially Dior. It comprised boned bodies and long, billowing, pleated skirts with tightly nipped-in waists, accessorized with a choker necklace and a large, tilted hat. Later collections were to develop a wide variety of popular styles, all of which showed unequalled elegance and a simple sculptural quality that influenced women's fashion over the following decades: jackets cut with upright collars and fly-away backs, slim skirts with a single pleat at the back, strapless evening gowns, and cropped and boxy jackets by the 1950s. Later years saw Dior's short version of the Princess-line jacket (full, round-shouldered and emphatically high-waisted) and the cone-shaped, low-browed coolie hat, with other styles typically featuring stoles and three-quarter length sleeves. Dior's 1952 three-piece pastel cardigan suit was widely influential as was his revamping of men's suiting in the mid-1950s, his ankle-length, figure-hugging sheath dresses and his bush jackets. He also spearheaded a revival of oriental tunic dresses towards the end of the decade.

After his death, Yves Saint Laurent took control of the Dior house. Design responsibility then passed to Marc Bohan, Gianfranco Ferré and latterly British designer John Galliano, who moved from Givenchy after only a year to take up the prestigious position.

Dolce & Gabbana

**Founders: Domenico Dolce & Stefano Gabbana
Born: Dolce – 1958, Sicily; Gabbana – 1962,
Milan, Italy**

Domenico Dolce and Stefano Gabbana's names have
come to represent a latter-day style of *la dolce vita*
glamour that has won fans from the worlds of theatre
and music (most notably Madonna, for whom the duo
has designed tour outfits) to the football terraces.

Domenico Dolce started designing for his father's atelier
business at a young age, whilst Stefano Gabbana turned to
fashion after studying graphic design. They both worked as
assistant designers for two years until a fluke meeting led to
them launching their own studio together in 1982.

Their big break came in 1985, when they were among
three names chosen to present collections in the 'new
talents' category at the Milan shows. They have never
looked back. Nor were they slow to grasp the dynamics of
business. Each year saw some new development that took
them closer to becoming a major global fashion brand.
Despite a recession, 1987 saw the launch of a knitwear line,
1988 an agreement with the Onward Kashiyama group for
distribution in Japan, 1989 the launch of their first lingerie
and beachwear line, and 1990 the arrival of Dolce &
Gabbana menswear. After a period designing the Complice
line for Genny, an Italian ready-to-wear company founded in
1961, they started to open their own shops in Europe and

Dolce

the Far East. In 1992 they launched an award-winning fragrance, which was followed by diffusion line Dolce & Gabbana Basic, the hugely successful D&G, bridalwear, homewares and a men's fragrance.

The essence of their design is an emphasis on their notion of a 'real' woman wearing their clothes: decidedly sensual, curvy, outfits for the boudoir that you could also wear outside, with an emphasis on lace, wool and silk, drawing inspiration from Mediterranean culture and colours. The duo had a more techno edge to their designs – unstructured clothing with tricky fastenings and hi-tech fabrics – before a trip to Sicily in 1987, which defined their signature attitude. The story goes that there they saw a poster of a woman, naked but for a black shawl. For them, the woman's strength and sexuality encapsulated their direction: womanliness in an age of wide-shouldered power-dressing.

Dolce & Gabbana's collections not only consistently make references to this Sicilian conversion – headscarves and rosary beads, full skirts, floral embroidery, gangster pinstripe suits for both men and women, bodices and empire-line dresses, peasant dressing and so on – but they were also notably central to the underwear-as-outerwear phenomenon of the late 1980s. The duo have been criticized by some for returning to a pre-feminist era style of dress, yet women in their droves continue to buy their garments.

&Gabbana

After 'underwear-as-outerwear', the next big style for Dolce & Gabbana was the gangster-style suit (1995), cut to flatter the female form

Salvatore Ferragamo

Founder: Salvatore Ferragamo
Born: 1898, Bonito, near Naples, Italy
Died: 1960, Flumetto, Italy

Born an émigré, and one of fourteen children, Salvatore Ferragamo arrived in Hollywood in the 1920s and made an immediate impact on its leading female stars, offering

Red satin high heels encrusted with rhinestones, made by Ferragamo for Marilyn Monroe, and auctioned by Christie's in 1999

beautiful, extravagant shoes that fit the anatomy of the foot. Gloria Swanson, Ava Gardner and Anna Magnani were among his many happy customers. Ferragamo had ambitions to make shoes from the age of nine, though it took a lot to convince his peasant father – who considered shoemaking a lowly profession – to allow him to move to Naples to begin an apprenticeship. In America, after a brief term making cowboy boots in a factory, he began work for the American Film Company, making imitations of Roman sandals for a series of Cecil B. de Mille epic films. A roster of private clients grew from this, some demanding a more rarefied version of the Roman sandal, which became his first signature design.

With business ever-growing, Ferragamo returned to Italy in 1927, establishing the centre of his operation in Florence. In the 1930s Ferragamo helped to introduce the wedge heel. He extended his handmade business by recruiting a team of shoemakers and introducing factory-made lines that sold in exclusive U.S. department stores during the 1950s. He also popularized platform soles and developed a metal support in towering high heels – just one of 20,000-plus different Ferragamo designs. He was a master at using unexpected materials such as raffia, needlework, snailshells, hemp and cellophane in his shoes (a development forced on him by wartime shortages). One of his most striking creations came in 1947: the 'invisible shoe', made from clear nylon on a black suede heel.

After Ferragamo's death, his business was developed by his wife Wanda, who introduced successful luxury ready-to-wear and men's lines.

Gianfranco Ferré

Founder: Gianfranco Ferré
Born: 1944, Legano, Italy

Gianfranco Ferré's reputation for simple-lined, bold, easy-to-wear womenswear has established the designer as a leading member of the Italian designer aristocracy. What perhaps sealed his reputation was his appointment as head of design for Christian Dior in 1989 (where he stayed until 1996).

Ferré qualified as an architect in Milan in 1969, joining the design studio of a furniture company. Some jewellery he designed and made for a girlfriend was seen by a boutique and led to an unexpected early career as an accessories designer, predominantly for Walter Albini and, from 1970, as a freelancer for Fiorucci and Karl Lagerfeld, among others. Ferré progressed from accessories in the mid-1970s to designing sportswear, which in turn led to the founding of his own fashion house and ready-to-wear line in 1978, with the sportier Oaks by Ferré line launched later the same year. He introduced his first women's fragrance in 1984. A men's fragrance and a couture collection followed in 1986.

Throughout the 1980s and 1990s his simple, strong suits were often favoured by women in executive jobs. He also brought back the big crinoline-supported ball gown.

Signature folding and layering of big, bold patterns on luxury fabrics as seen at Ferré's autumn/winter shows in 1999

Fiorucci

Founder: Elio Fiorucci
Born: 1935, Milan, Italy

Fiorucci is perhaps more synonymous with fashion concepts than fashion design. Once a family business, now owned by a number of multi-national corporations, the skill of this company lies in its ability to recycle other designers' styles and looks and make something fun and fashionable from them – to appropriate and give them new meanings.

The Fiorucci business began when, at 22, Elio Fiorucci – new head of a small Milanese handmade shoe business, just inherited from his father – took three pairs of brightly coloured galoshes to the local fashion magazine and persuaded it to print a photograph of them. Suddenly, Fiorucci had a fashion phenomenon on his hands, one in contrast to the strict conservativism of standard Italian dress of the time.

From then on, the company went from strength to strength, tapping into cultural movements, borrowing ideas and selling the products that came out of them, be they parachute-cloth jumpsuits in pink and yellow, or traditional workman's lunchboxes turned into handbags. By the 1970s, Fiorucci was a world-famous name, opening stores across the planet, each one as innovative in its presentation and packaging as the youth-orientated products it sold.

The brand's skill was always in the details: in the choice of bright buttons for a man's shirt, or a metallic thread running through an otherwise sober fabric. In addition, although not original in its designs – its most popular item during the 1970s was a pair of streamlined jeans – Fiorucci can be held responsible for creating some of fashion's key trends of the past four decades: fishnet stockings, *faux* animal skin fabrics, jelly shoes (brightly coloured plastic sandals), the use of military fabrics, gold lamé and Lycra. Similarly, Fiorucci was responsible for bringing the work of many other designers to Italy, notably that of Ossie Clark, Betsy Johnson and Jim O'Connor, of the influential London fashion shop Mr Freedom.

A number of designs made Fiorucci's name in the 1970s and 1980s, but perhaps the most famous was the jelly shoe. Although it had been worn for years by children, the house revolutionized the shoe by putting it on grown-ups

John Galliano

Founder: John Galliano
Born: 1960, Gibraltar

Artist? Showman? Historian? All are labels that can readily be applied to the flamboyant John Galliano, a British designer with a reputation for craftsmanship and romanticism in his work. Born to an English father and Spanish mother, Galliano moved to London when he was six years old. He quit school at the age of sixteen to learn fabric design at East London College, progressing to London's Central Saint Martins College of Art and Design. From there, he graduated in 1984 with first-class honours and a commercially minded collection of garments entitled 'Les Incroyables', based on styles from the French Revolution. These designs were already true to Galliano's signature style of extensive and exacting historical referencing, from African dress to Berlin cabaret and film stars of the 1930s and 1940s.

Galliano's next collection employed Mohican motifs and was entitled 'Afghanistan Repudiates Western Ideals'. It confirmed both his taste for the eccentric, and the already obvious fact that he was a designer of considerable talent and a force to be reckoned with in the fashion world. Galliano is also technically inventive: he favours bias-cutting techniques and has soaked silk chiffon in gelatine to create a crumpled look, made L-shaped dresses, hidden jacket lapels and produced dresses supported by telephone wire. His

subsequent collections have tackled clothes as diverse as crinolines and kilts, frockcoats and gangster-style suits.

Galliano moved to Paris in 1991. In 1995 he was offered a job by Bernard Arnault, chairman of the luxury brand conglomerate Louis Vuitton Moet Hennessy. This secured his status as one of the leading designers of his generation, and he was appointed designer for Givenchy. Galliano only stayed for two collections before moving on to design for Christian Dior. Alexander McQueen filled his shoes at Givenchy. Galliano did the trick for Dior, putting the flagging name back into the fashion headlines. He created widely imitated, highly glamorous, tight-waisted suits teamed with gigantic necklaces, shawl dresses and long sensuous gowns worn at awards ceremonies by stars like actress Nicole Kidman.

Galliano's appointment at Dior was regarded with some suspicion, and he has not been without his critics. However, whilst his haute couture shows remain high on invention and low on wearability, no one denies the pure artistry and sensational originality of Galliano's couture. His 2000 spring/summer show was inspired by the down-and-outs of Paris, deconstructing and then reconstructing traditional couture garments to create ragged, but structurally unique, outfits. Crazed ballerinas, bundled ball-dresses and slashed suits strutted down the catwalks – beautifully lunatic, the show reached new levels of performance art.

Glamorous updated kilts for the year 2000, Galliano-style. For some, his designs have become a little too outrageous

Jean-Paul Gaultier

Founder: Jean-Paul Gaultier
Born: 1952, Paris, France

Frequently referred to as the 'enfant terrible' of Paris fashion, Jean-Paul Gaultier has made a career out of constant changes of direction. His designs have veered from referencing the religious to the hedonistic, the sexy to the prim, the unisex to the voluptuously feminine or macho masculine, and have found their inspiration variously in the 1970s punk movement, street style and Gaultier's infamous and endless scouring of flea markets.

Gaultier was obsessed with fashion from a young age. He began sketching at fourteen and sent sketches out to designers at the age of seventeen. His grandmother taught him make-up, hairdressing and dressmaking, though his break into the fashion world proper came when he was hired by Pierre Cardin to work on couture. Gaultier then worked for Jacques Estrel, Jean Patou before returning to Cardin (to work at his operation in the Philippines), leaving again to produce his first collection in 1977. After several years Gaultier found financial backing from the Japanese Kashiyama Group in 1979 (and Gibo and Equator of Italy), leading to a collection based on

James Bond. Gaultier's clothes mix glamour with wit and old with new, and they have been both challenging and influential. He has used mini Eiffel Towers as shoe heels, made bustiers and skirts for men, defined a look for a modern-day dandy and was one of the designers behind the underwear-as-outerwear phenomenon of the mid-1980s. He has been central to fashion's emphasis on the bustline in the latter part of the century. Needless to say, Madonna is a big fan.

Such are Gaultier's talents that he was widely tipped to replace Gianfranco Ferré as head of design at Dior in 1996, but the job eventually went to John Galliano. His ability to tap into so many styles has brought him much high-profile work outside the usual fashion arena. He designed the costumes for Peter Greenaway's film *The Cook, The Thief, His Wife and Her Lover* (1989) and those pointy-breasted corsets for Madonna on her Blonde Ambition tour, and even more unusually he co-hosted (with Antoine de Caunes) the British TV show *Eurotrash*.

Madonna's Blonde Ambition tour, 1990. One of the defining moments for 1990s fashion and the point at which Gaultier became a household name. Often by using the old, Gaultier manages to stay thoroughly modern

Gaultier

Romeo Gigli

Founder: Romeo Gigli
Born: 1951, Bologna, Italy

Western fashion's love of ethnic Eastern dress finds its most refined and delicate form in the designs of Romeo Gigli. Romance, luxury, understatement and sensuality are his bywords, with the emphasis on clothes and stretch fabrics (as well as chiffon, silk, linen and cashmere) that fit the lines of the body, along with classical gentle draping, asymmetry, embroidery and velvet. Colours are deep and rich, from dark blue to soft pink, mole brown and moss green. Basics include tunic knits, narrow trousers and long, fitted jackets. Despite this subtlety, Gigli's entry into the fashion world in 1986 came like a bomb, his style contrasting so sharply with the square-shouldered power-dressing of the time.

Romeo Gigli was born into an aristocratic family. Having studied architecture for a short time, he was drawn to fashion, perhaps under the influence of his father's books, gathered throughout the East (which clearly figures in Gigli's designs). Indeed, Gigli has stated that his muses include the Empress Theodora from Byzantium and the Virgins of Piero della Francesca. He began designing in 1972, setting up his own label in 1983. But he really took off after a business restructuring in 1991, following a split from business partners Donato Maiano and Carla Sozzani. In 1991, the prestigious Bath Costume house chose a Gigli midnight-blue velvet trouser suit as its Dress of the Year.

Deep, rich colour and luxurious stretch fabrics define both the look and the feel of Gigli's designs. He is perhaps most famous for his tunic knits, worn with tight trousers (1988)

Givenchy

Founder: Hubert Givenchy
Born: 1927, Beauvais, France

Hubert Givenchy's career in fashion nearly failed to get off the ground. His parents had plans for him to be a lawyer, and for a family that had made its money through mining, fashion was not regarded as an acceptable profession. He pushed on regardless, working for Jacques Fath in the post-war years until 1949, and then under Elsa Schiaparelli before going it alone.

Givenchy opened his own fashion house in 1952. His first collection was a simple one of clean-lined formal elegance, focusing on evening dresses and based around pleated cotton skirts and blouses from organdy, a light cotton, chemically-stiffened fabric used chiefly as a trimming for dresses. The collection also introduced the widely copied 'Bettina' blouse, made from men's shirting fabric, with huge ruffled sleeves, and named after Bettina Graziani, one of the top models of the time. Nevertheless, it was acclaimed as a welcome departure from Dior's 'New Look'. Later collections showed a flair for adaptable clothes; for instance, his evening

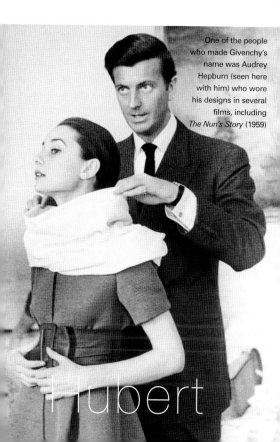

One of the people who made Givenchy's name was Audrey Hepburn (seen here with him) who wore his designs in several films, including *The Nun's Story* (1959)

Hubert

dress with bodice, which could be removed and worn instead with trousers or a different skirt.

But, as so often happens with new designers, it was patronage that brought international success. Audrey Hepburn wore a Givenchy dress in Billy Wilder's film *Sabrina* (1954) and, following the development of a close friendship between the two, wore Givenchy again in the films *Funny Face* (1957), *Charade* (1963), *Love in the Afternoon* (1957) and *Breakfast at Tiffany's* (1961). The clothes showed off Hepburn's figure, with the shallow bateau neckline in particular emphasizing her shoulders. The designer could not have hoped for a better advertisement for his skills. Givenchy's clothes for Hepburn were hugely influential then and remain so today.

Givenchy sold his business in 1988, although he continued to design and head the company until his retirement in 1996. In that year, the young Brit Alexander McQueen was made head of design, replacing John Galliano.

In 1995, a year before his retirement, Givenchy was still defining sophistication with his black-bodiced evening dress

Grès

Founder: Germaine Emilie Krebs
Born: 1903, Paris, France
Died: 1993, France

Like so many other designers at the turn of the century, Germaine Emilie Krebs's parents were not keen on her following a career in painting and sculpture, her great interests. But fashion seemed like a happy compromise.

Krebs began her fashion career designing 'toiles' (muslin-made garment patterns), which she sold on to Paris fashion houses. She worked for the house of Premet (which closed in 1931) and finally began her own business under the Alix Barton name in Paris in 1934. The house of Grès was established in 1942 after the German occupation. Madame Grès managed to put out just one collection before the house was closed down for flamboyantly using the red, white and blue of the French flag throughout her designs. However, this was enough to establish at least the business's name: Grès, taken from the anagram used by her painter husband Serge Cezrefkov. She reopened the house after World War II, and it quickly became popular with theatre and cinema stars. Grace Kelly and Jackie Kennedy were among her keen customers. The essentially classic designs of Grès specialized in draping and precisely pleated evening gowns, dolman sleeves (the type with a deep armhole that may extend as far as the waist) and bias-cutting, and typically employed jersey, wool and silk.

Business continued steadily until the French businessman Bernard Tapie bought the company in 1984. Liquidation followed and the company was bought by the Japanese Yagi Tsusho corporation, upon which Madame Grès retired. She became a recluse until her death – strangely, an event only revealed to the rest of Grès's family and to the world media by her daughter Anne the following year. The house now continues under the designer Frederic Molenac and has been widely tipped for a major revival.

The dolman sleeves, draping and pleating of Grès's evening gowns (seen here in 1965) are all expected to return this century

Grès

Gucci

Founder: Guccio Gucci
Born: 1881, Florence, Italy
Died: 1953, Milan, Italy

Gucci was one of the first Italian brand names to be known worldwide. The products that have become synonymous with the name – the duffel bag of 1925, the loafer with the signature snaffle-bit of 1932 as worn by John Wayne, the handbag with the bamboo handle, among others – became fashion classics in the 1950s. And with the 1950s came expansion to New York (in 1953), and then London, Palm Beach, Paris, Beverly Hills and Tokyo. But this move beyond Italy also caused the first family infighting, culminating in the contract killing of Maurizio Gucci by his wife in 1998.

The son of a craftsman, Guccio moved to Paris when he was young (after a family squabble), working his way up to become the maitre d' at the Savoy. It was there that he spotted the guests' love of luxury – notably simple, classical, stylish goods. So, back in Italy in 1920, he opened the first Gucci shop in Florence, selling leather goods and riding accessories. With his sons – Aldo, Vasco, Ugo and Rodolfo – involved, growth was steady, and shops opened in Rome and Milan. The opening of the first shop outside Italy met with fervent objections from Guccio. He died the same year.

By the following decade, Audrey Hepburn, Jackie Kennedy and other members of the beau monde had bought into the lifestyle. Factories opened, success seemed assured,

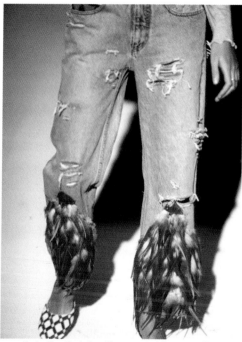

Under Tom Ford, Gucci has extended the range of its
designs to include less formal garments, such as
feathered and jewelled jeans (1999)

Tom Ford

but the family fought on. The company struggled through the 1970s and early 1980s, and Rodolfo's son Maurizio was made group president in 1989. On the advice of Dawn Mello, brought in from New York store Bergdorf Goodman, production was cut back from 20,000 items to a core of 5000 classics; and the distribution was reduced. This fitted in with the Gucci motto: 'Stay small to remain great'.

Maurizio ran the company until 1993, when it was close to bankruptcy. Family members were jailed for tax evasion. Others fought over the company's direction. Maurizio sold his part of the business to Arab multinational Investcorp, which then acquired the business in its entirety. It wasn't the end of an era, however, but the start of a reinvention that, by the late 1990s, had made Gucci one of the world's most desirable fashion brands. Under Investcorp, in 1994, a little-known 36-year-old American studio assistant called Tom Ford was appointed creative director.

Ford had studied at New York University, quitting to act in TV commercials. Not making it as an actor, he attended New York's Parsons School of Design to study fashion and interior design. He then worked for designers Cathy Handwick and Perry Ellis, and joined Gucci in 1990. Here Ford produced a marketing phenomenon. Out went tradition and in came sex: leather, revealing cut-out dresses, towering metallic stilettos and the style that made Ford's name: velvet hipsters. Ad campaigns sold this new mood, suggesting something sexual – a ménage à trois or lesbian encounter – going on below the surface. At the time of writing, Ford combines his work at Gucci with his new appointment as creative director at Yves Saint Laurent.

Since the mid-1990s, Gucci has been hindered only by economic problems in the Far East– one of the company's key markets – and competition from another Italian brand that has undergone a similarly brilliant image and product overhaul: Prada. Indeed, Prada now owns a large shareholding in Gucci.

Halston

Founder: Roy Halston Frowick
Born: 1932, Iowa, U.S.A.
Died: 1990, San Francisco, U.S.A.

Roy Halston Frowick achieved fame predominantly in the late 1970s, during the Studio 54 days of wild partying, although he was already an established designer with a loyal clientele. After attending the University of Indiana and the Chicago Institute, he opened his first business in 1953. Specializing in millinery and based in a Chicago hotel (later to move to French milliner Lilly Dache, she of the towering fruit-covered Carmen Miranda turbans, and then to Bergdorf Goodman, both in New York), he quickly attracted the attentions of Deborah Kerr, Gloria Swanson and other actresses of the time. Later he would also design for Jackie Kennedy, notably a felt pill-box hat.

Halston began designing ready-to-wear in 1966, when he left Bergdorf Goodman. He specialized in knits – sweaters, halter-neck dresses that became a big hit with the glam disco crowd, sweater sets and jersey trousers (especially using matt jersey). Two of his creations particularly captured the imagination: tie-dyed chiffon and a knee-length shirt-dress in Ultrasuede.

Jackie Kennedy at JFK's inauguration ceremony, wearing the 'pill-box' hat which was to make Halston's name

Katharine Hamnett

Founder: Katherine Hamnett
Born: 1948, Gravesend, Kent, England

In 1983 Katharine Hamnett made a particular type of fashion statement; she launched her 'Choose Life' T-shirt collection, of plain white Ts with big, bold and black political statements, among them 'Stop acid rain', 'Preserve the rain forests' and '58% don't want Pershing', which Hamnett famously wore at a meeting with the then British prime minister Margaret Thatcher. Despite being copied with considerably more diluted messages (notably by 1980s bands Wham and Frankie Goes to Hollywood), the T-shirts made a contribution towards raising political awareness at the time.

But 1983 was more than the year of the T-shirt for Hamnett. The same year saw the launch of her London menswear and denim collections which, together, secured her worldwide business and contributed to her winning of the coveted British Fashion Council Designer of the Year award. She

Katharine Hamnett, best known outside fashion circles for her slogan T-shirts, circa 1983

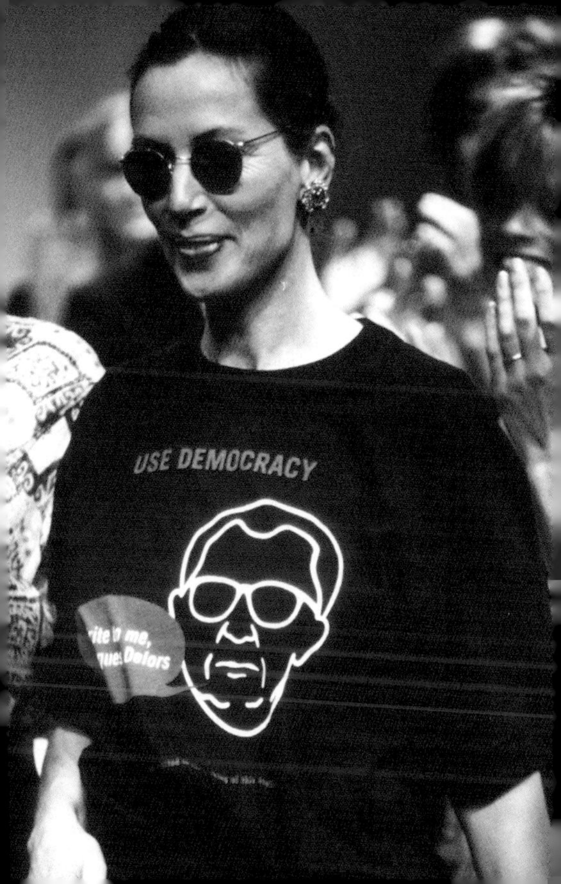
USE DEMOCRACY

began by attending Central Saint Martins College of Art and Design in London, graduating in 1970 to freelance internationally for a number of clothing companies. Hamnett set up on her own in 1979, initially influenced by workwear from around the world and – a fashion first – using padded silk for outerwear. Other innovations included distressed denim in 1985 and condom pockets on boxer shorts in 1986. An eclectic designer, Hamnett's work has also included strong tailoring – in Britain she was at the forefront of power-dressing in the 1980s – and Pre-Raphaelite styles (including tea-dresses), jodhpurs and designs for the Ballet Rambert.

Leading fashion's scant interest in politics, Hamnett's environmental concerns in particular have extended from using minimal packaging, to using 'green' fabrics such as organic cotton, Tencel and Wensleydale wool and banning the use of PVC. Hamnett has also distributed political information at her shows and used the very name of the shows as a consciousness-raising device, notably at 1990's 'Cancel the Third World Debt' show and 'Green Cotton by the Year 2000' show in 1991. She has also given speeches on subjects such as the dangers of conventional cotton cultivation. Her brand name extends to watches, shoes and eyewear.

Much of the 1990s was a more sensual, celebratory time for Hamnett's designs, with garments such as her black and gold stretch evening dress

Marc Jacobs

Designer: Marc Jacobs
Born: 1960, New York, U.S.A.

Marc Jacobs studied at New York's High School of Art and Design and then Parsons School of Design. He designed for Reuben Thomas before launching his own label with Robert Duffy in 1986. He then won the CFDA (Council for Fashion Designers of America) New Fashion Talent award – he was the youngest designer to do so – and joined Perry Ellis in 1988. Here he designed influential, often irreverent clothes, notably his red gingham dress with embroidered black ants.

In the summer of 1993, Jacobs created a fashion sensation with his collection for Perry Ellis, showing women in sloppy sweaters and chunky army boots, outsize flannel shirts and floral, vintage-inspired dresses. Grunge was born. But for every reaction that praised this way of dress which gave women more freedom, there was a refusal to spend over a thousand dollars on a dress that looked second-hand. Grunge may have been a fashion triumph, but it was a business disaster. Although the collection arguably won Jacobs the prestigious CFDA Best Womenswear Designer Award of 1993, the 35-year-old designer – ironically best-known for his clean, pared-down sportswear – was fired by Perry Ellis the following year. Grunge, however, lived on, a rare example of a style that looks as though it came from the street, but actually originated on the catwalk.

After Perry Ellis, Jacobs returned to designing his own

sportswear line, with his 1994 collection of hooded tweed jackets, sequinned skirts and red and green leather tops, receiving rave reviews. Such was the interest in his collection that Bernard Arnault, head of the Louis Vuitton Moet Hennessy (LVMH) conglomerate, invited Jacobs to join the company as artistic director, to design its fledgling ready-to-wear collections. Jacobs has been so successful with the brand – one of several old-school luxury brands reinvented over the 1990s, including Hermès, Gucci and Prada – that he won the CFDA Best Womenswear Designer award again in 1998.

Charles Jourdan

Founder: Charles Jourdan
Born: 1883, France
Died: 1976, Romans sur Isère, France

Although Charles Jourdan died over thirty years ago, his name remains synonymous with contemporary, conservative and desirable footwear. Jourdan was designing elegant women's shoes before World War II disrupted business, so it was only after the war, when he was joined in the business by his three sons, that the name took off.

In 1921, early in his career, Jourdan started a show workshop in Romans, in France's Drome region and quickly built up a successful if small-scale business. The first shop opened in Paris in 1957, with the breakthrough coming in 1959, when the house of Dior granted Jourdan a licence to make its shoes. Although Jourdan's shoes are classic, the company's image has always been cutting-edge, with an eye for current styling.

Two styles in particular managed to remaining distinctly Jourdan whilst reflecting the trends of the day – a low, square-toed court shoe with a satin bow in the 1960s, and a red and black patent leather platform in the 1970s. At the end of the 1960s the Man Ray-influenced photographer Guy Bourdin, a French *Vogue* regular, was hired to maintain the tradition by shooting Jourdan's ad campaign.

By the end of his career, Jourdan was working for fashion giant Dior as well as for Xavier Danaud and Pierre Cardin.

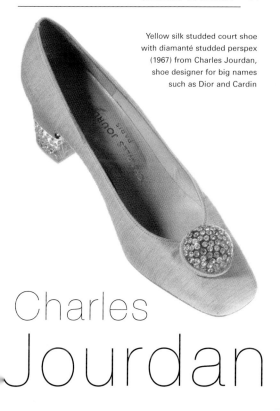

Yellow silk studded court shoe with diamanté studded perspex (1967) from Charles Jourdan, shoe designer for big names such as Dior and Cardin

Charles
Jourdan

Founder: Donna Karan
Born: 1948, New York, U.S.A.

Donna Karan was surrounded by fashion from the start, with her mother a model and her father a haberdasher. She studied at Parsons School of Design in New York, along with Isaac Mizrahi and photographer Steven Meisel, but left after her second year when she was offered a full-time job while on an internship at Anne Klein. A driven businesswoman as well as a skilful designer, by 1969 Karan was named as Klein's successor. By 1971 she was associate designer and in 1974, after Klein's death, she was made head of the company. Then, in 1984, after ten years of designing with Luis dell'Olio (who, with Klein, was instrumental in creating the easy sportswear look which dominates Karan's own collections), Karan left Klein to launch her own label.

Karan's $600-million business stems from the simplest of design approaches. The New York designer/brand name only designs what she herself likes to wear, leading to a collection based around dark blue or black, comfort and separates which the wearer can mix and match. The designs often use stretch and draped fabrics and are sympathetic to non-model figures.

This has been Karan's approach from the very beginning: her first collection, in 1984, was based around a wraparound skirt and a black bodysuit, the

latter wearable with everything from jeans to a suit. Perhaps Karan has not established a reputation for breaking new ground in fashion, but the functionality of her clothes has made her the epitome of understated cosmopolitan New York style. The fact that her clothes are often worn by close friends Demi Moore and Barbra Streisand has also guaranteed her the kind of publicity that money can't buy.

Karan's artistic success can be measured by the awards she has stacked up over the years: among other trophies, the Council for Fashion Designers of America named her best designer in 1985, 1990, 1992 and 1997. Her business skills have also paid dividends: as well as becoming an established name in womenswear, Karan has launched menswear, the successful DKNY diffusion line, and homewares, fragrances, hosiery and cosmetics.

Donna

Kara

Donna Karan's name was made in the 1990s due to the 'wearability' of designs such as her black body suit with wrap-around skirt (1999)

Kenzo

Founder: Kenzo Takada
Born: 1939, Kyoto, Japan

Best known for his bright prints and layering, Kenzo Takada
found immediate success when he opened his first shop,
Jungle Jap, in 1970. By 1972, Jungle Jap was well established
with a signature style of tunics, smocks, wide-legged
trousers, oriental influences, velvet garments, mixed patterns
(such as combinations of tartan and stripes) and especially
knitwear. Other innovations included the use of 100 per
cent cotton fabrics (even in winter), enlarged armholes and
new, soft shoulder shapes.

All Kenzo's collections are influenced by the designer's
wide travels – Mao jackets from China, Aztec-style shawls,
Romanian peasant dress or dresses worn over trousers, as in
Vietnam – and mix extensive references. But they have one
distinct and enduring motif: flowers. These reflect Kenzo's
Japanese flower-arranging heritage and echo his use of
vibrant colour, going against strong trends elsewhere for
monocolour and clear seasonal variation.

Kenzo's name has stayed in the spotlight because he mixes
and matches styles and influences from all over the world
and makes them his own, sometimes by fashioning colourful
ethnic fabrics into dresses, and sometimes (*see over*) by
using them as simple wraps

Born one of seven children, Kenzo studied literature at Kobe Gaibo University, which went against his own desire to study fashion, but satisfied his parents' wishes. He lasted a term before leaving to move to Tokyo. There, he worked as an apprentice house painter before, in 1958, getting a place at the Bunka Fashion College. On graduation Kenzo not only designed patterns for magazines on a freelance basis but was hired to design for the Sanai department store. It wasn't until he moved to Paris in 1965 – financed by a compensation windfall after the building he lived in was demolished – that Kenzo's fashion career really took off. He started by selling designs to Louis Féraud, then to several department stores, including Pisanti. Once his own business began, Kenzo quickly developed a distinct style – his 1977 collection introduced long, wide jackets, while the 1978 collection turned to short jackets with short, wide trousers, proportions that were notably influential during the 1980s – and a fast expanding business.

From 1984 to 1985 some ten Kenzo boutiques were opened around the world. The business now also encompasses Kenzo Homme (established in 1983), Kenzo Jeans, Enfant (1997) and Bébé, homewares (1992) and fragrances. He has also designed for the theatre and opera, and a teaching chair at Paris's Ecole des Beaux-Arts was named after him in 1990. The company was acquired by LVMH in 1993. Kenzo announced his departure from fashion design in September of 1999, an announcement that coincided with the founding of a Kenzo Style School. Kenzo in-house designers Gilles Rosier and Roy Krejberg took over responsibilities for women's and menswear respectively.

Calvin Klein

Founder: Calvin Klein
Born: 1942, New York, U.S.A.

The secret of Calvin Klein's clothes is their simplicity and wearability and yet the name of Calvin Klein is complex in its significance. Klein is a household name, an aspiration as much as a label. King of sportswear, Klein has consistently worked his collections to offer a minimalist, practical and unfussy wardrobe of wearable clothes in a neutral palette and, often, luxury linen, silk and woollen fabrics. But this simplicity belies his skill: Klein has been so much more than the boxer shorts with which he made his name.

Born in the Bronx, he went on to study at New York High School of Art and Design and then joined the Fashion Institute of Technology, graduating in 1962. Klein spent two years as assistant designer with Dan Millstein in New York and from 1964 he worked for a variety of dressmakers, before starting a women's coat business with friend (and now Chief Executive Officer of Calvin Klein Inc) Barry Schwartz in 1968. With a shift to strong sportswear from the mid-1970s, Klein quickly found his signature.

Collections have included often unisex, updated staples such as turtleneck sweaters, loose long-line trousers, pea-coats, blousey shirt-jackets, blazers and loose jackets. Indeed, above and beyond his clothes (which, despite their seeming anonymity are distinctly Klein's), what Klein has understood, perhaps above all designers, is the importance

Calvin Klein
and Kate Moss

Calvin Klein is famous not only for his underwear but also for designing garments which look unisex. In his autumn/winter 1999 collection this took the form of grey minimalism

of the lifestyle package – an understanding that has made him a favourite of the Hollywood set.

Klein's advertising has been consistently effective in giving a mainstream stylish product a more edgy allure. It has been daring (a cK Jeans ad in 1995 was retracted, following accusations of child pornography) and always in tune with the zeitgeist – be it Brooke Shields revealing that 'nothing gets between me and my Calvins', actor and then boyband member Mark Wahlberg posing in his boxer shorts (and spreading a trend for branded underwear elastic to be highly visible above trousers), a long association with model Kate Moss for his Obsession campaigns, or the abandoning of models in favour of putting 'real' rock'n'rollers Shirley Manson and Jon Spencer in his ads.

By the same token, Klein has been a master of brand extension. His name is now also applied to menswear, his cK diffusion line, footwear, watches, eyewear, notably successful fragrances (especially cKOne, certainly at one point the world's best-selling fragrance) and, of course, underwear. He is widely credited with 'inventing' designer jeans in the 1970s, and certainly his version was widely copied.

In 1993 he won the Council of Fashion designers of America's awards for Best Womenswear and Best Menswear designer. In 1999 he put his company on the market.

Christian Lacroix

Founder: Christian Lacroix
Born: 1951, Arles, France

Christian Lacroix studied art history at Montpellier University before moving to Paris to train as a museum curator at the Ecole du Louvre. There he designed opera costumes which he showed to Saint Laurent's partner Pierre Berge and to Karl Lagerfeld.

Lacroix launched his haute couture house on Paris's rue Faubourg St Honoré in 1987, during an economic recession. That first collection brought a revival of couture's former glory: brightly coloured baroque, almost theatrical, costumes based around crinolines, some topped off with powdered wigs. Although the collection received mixed reviews, Lacroix sold 20 dresses over the next two years. This represented good business at $75,000 apiece. From here on the house of Lacroix went from strength to strength. It included the pouf dress (puffed-out and tucked-up at the back), ostentatious capes, a brazen mix of prints, bright colours, the asymmetric and the babydoll and a range of branded products (notably perfumes and the Bazar range of more accessibly priced Lacroix clothes).

Lacroix is known for his bullfighter jackets which are heavily inspired by theatrical costume (1999)

Karl

Karl Lagerfeld

Founder: Karl Lagerfeld
Born: 1939, Hamburg, Germany

Legend has it that Karl Lagerfeld began sketching when his mother, by all accounts a brilliant, multi-talented woman who overshadowed young Karl's privileged childhood, grew tired of his piano-playing and advised him to draw instead because it made less noise. His talent was quickly evident.

Having moved to Paris 1952, it took two years for Lagerfeld to win his first competition: the coat category of the Woolmark Design Competition (a young Yves Saint Laurent won the dress design prize in the same competition). In 1956, Lagerfeld joined Pierre Balmain as a designer (it was Balmain who put his winning coat design into production), moving to Jean Patou as creative director at the age of just 20. In 1964 he left fashion to study art in Italy, but returned to fashion the following year.

From the mid-1960s Lagerfeld worked freelance, establishing himself as a leading light in the fashion world. His portfolio includes stints at many of the leading names in dressy fashion, designing acclaimed collections at a prolific rate and injecting new lifeblood from behind his signature personal style: dark suit, dark sunglasses, ponytail and fan. Indeed, his dress echoes his outspoken attitude and fashion-world reputation as a man not to be crossed. He made Claudia Schiffer into a supermodel, but within a few years was just as quick to condemn her look as old news.

Krizia, Chloé, Ballantyne knitwear, Valentino and Jourdan shoes all received the sophisticated and confident Lagerfeld touch. From 1967 he designed for Fendi, where he established himself as one of the most innovative designers to work with fur – particularly when transforming unfashionable squirrel and rabbit fur by dyeing it with vibrant brights and creating a reversible fur coat. From 1983, Lagerfeld became design director for Chanel. He can take the bulk of the credit for making Chanel into the revival story of the 1980s. In 1984 Lagerfeld, also a talented stylist, photographer and artist, launched his own line. His scope has been broad, encompassing bodices, skirts worn over trousers, kimonos, mini-skirts and, often, his signature long fitted jacket.

One aspect of Lagerfeld's designs that singles him out is his skill as an artist. His bright striped dress of 1995 showed his confidence with colour

Helmut Lang

Founder: Helmut Lang
Born: 1956, Vienna, Austria

By the end of the 1990s, Helmut Lang had established strong positions in two very opposite camps. With strong ready-to-wear catwalk collections, precise tailoring, advanced fabrics in a dark, stark palette and a quirky edginess, Lang was respected as a designer of crisp, modern, essentially deconstructed, unisex clothing. By the same token, his Jeans label, making its big impact in 1998, appealed to the new urban, functional fashion and offered updated work shirts (distinguished by a contrasting stripe of material), re-styled Mod parkas and simple, narrow-legged trousers.

This duality reflects the forward thinking, cleverly constructed nature of his essentially urban clothes, and the kind of street-wise yet elegant creature he designs for, and the multi-function lives they lead.

Lang launched his own fashion business in 1977. A number of flagship stores, notably in Munich, Vienna, Milan and New York followed.

Helmut Lang has made his name by redefining old ideas, a classic example being his updated Mod parka jacket (1999)

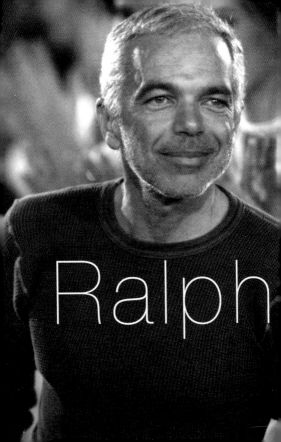

Ralph Lauren

Founder: Ralph Lauren
Born: 1939, New York, U.S.A.

The power of Ralph Lauren's brand has almost superseded his status as a designer. Beginning with a humble tie range under the Polo brand in 1967, Lauren's brands now encompass everything from fragrances to duvet covers (he was also the first fashion designer to launch paints and wall-finishes) and a host of global brands: Polo, Ralph, Purple Label, Lauren, Polo Jeans Co., Polo Sport and so on.

Since the Polo menswear company was established in 1968, Lauren has been widely influential with his gentrified Ivy League style of croquet-lawn casualwear – blending the romance and tradition of East Coast college-style button-down shirts, narrow-shouldered loose jackets, heavy Oxford shoes, with women in twinsets, blazers, Bermuda shorts and brogues. Indeed, his look has become the hallmark of American dressing, from upper-class white-collar management to street-teen hip-hop crews. It was Lauren's groundbreaking brand-building that made the globally successful, sporty brand Tommy Hilfiger possible.

He first worked at Brooks Brothers in New York as a glove salesman while studying business at City College nightschool. In 1967 he joined Beau Brummel Neckwear, where the Polo brand was later created to launch an exclusive tie range. After extending his tie label to menswear, womenswear followed in 1971. This was followed by the Ralph Lauren label in 1972. This consisted of essentially updated classic items, such as pleated skirts, hacking jackets, the much-copied prairie look of denim skirts worn over white petticoats in 1978, an American frontier style extended in 1980 with full skirts, and ruffled linen blouses.

Huge business success – over 100 stores worldwide, with the first opening in Beverly Hills in 1971, and his shop in London in 1981 making Lauren the first American designer with a store in Europe; the first flagship store opened in the famous Rhinelander Mansion on New York's Madison avenue in 1986 – has been matched by critical accolades. He remains, for instance, the only designer to receive all five of the Council of Fashion Designers of America's awards: for retail, womenswear, menswear, humanitarian leadership (notably for support of breast cancer and AIDS research), and the coveted lifetime achievement award. The small and oft illegally-copied embroidered Polo Pony (first used on a woman's shirt in 1971) has become one of the world's most recognized brands.

Variations on the lacy petticoat theme have been a part of Lauren's designs since 1978, including the flower-embroidered top featured in his spring/summer 1998 collection

Lauren

Martin Margiela

Founder: Martin Margiela
Born: 1957, Louvain, Belgium

Martin Margiela attended Antwerp's Royal Academy of Fine Art along with designers Dries van Noten, Ann Demeulemeester, Dirk Van Saene, Walter van Beirendonck of Wild & Lethal Trash, and Dirk Bikkembergs. On graduation he worked as a stylist before moving to Paris in 1982 to work with Gaultier. He left in 1988 to start his own business, La Maison Martin Margiela, showing his first solo collection the following year to widespread critical acclaim.

Margiela is regarded as one of the most conceptual of fashion designers, in the vein of Comme des Garçons' Rei Kawakubo. He is an ardent developer of new construction techniques – exposed linings, external seams, slashed sleeves, opposing textures and unusual mixed materials (from antique tulle to plastic). However, his hallmark is the perfect finish to unusual pieces – his ripped sleeve jackets are beautifully made. His summer 1997 collection took this paradox to its extreme, and revealed the rough foundations of high fashion by using tailor's dummy markings and pattern-cutting fabric.

He has designed clothes patterned with bacterial mould, made tops from broken dishes and printed photographic

A speciality of Margiela is laying construction techniques bare, as he did with the chalk-marked suits of his 1997 collection

Martin

images of heavy sweaters and fur coats onto light crepe dresses. To add to the deconstructionist label he has also earned associations with the flea-market grunge aesthetic for contrasting the new with the old, the hard with the soft – making sweaters from heavy-duty army socks.

Even Margiela's catwalk collections have often been theatrical: collections have been shown in car parks and on the Paris Metro, models have been dispensed with in favour of slide shows, men in white lab coats have carried the collection down the catwalk and, perhaps most radically, a new collection has not been shown at all. Instead a 'best of' review of past collections was shown – only everything was dyed the same battleship grey. Perhaps unsurprisingly, Margiela's mystique extends beyond his design. In contrast with most publicity-hungry designers, he refuses to be photographed or interviewed and his name is absent from his garments. Each piece has a label, but it's blank.

Yet Margiela's designs are wearable. His appointment in April 1997 to head womenswear design at Hermès was regarded by many as an April Fool's joke. But his first collection, shown in March 1998, proved even the most sceptical wrong. Although conventional by Margiela's standards, it included many garments that mixed his own preferences for construction detail with the kind of luxury materials typical of Hermès.

Margiela

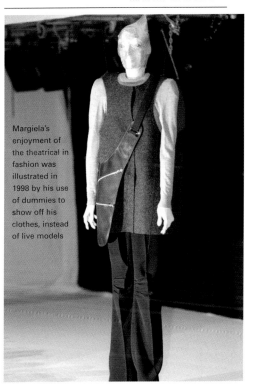

Margiela's enjoyment of the theatrical in fashion was illustrated in 1998 by his use of dummies to show off his clothes, instead of live models

Claire McCardell

Founder: Claire McCardell
Born: 1905, Maryland, U.S.A.
Died: 1958, New York, U.S.A.

Without the work of Claire McCardell, it's perhaps no exaggeration to say that 'sportswear', the American term for loose, comfortable, versatile daywear, would not have made fortunes for the likes of Donna Karan and Calvin Klein. Certainly, although no longer a household name, McCardell is widely considered to be one of the most influential American designers.

McCardell studied at the Hood College before moving to New York in 1927 to attend the Parsons School of Design. After a Parisian interlude, she returned to New York, sketching for dress shops on a freelance basis before joining designer Richard Turk in 1929. When he moved to Townley Frocks in 1931, she followed, taking over his position when he died not long afterwards. Subsequent moves took her to Hattie Carnegie (designer of simple, conventional, but much-desired dresses and skirts, often in what became known as Carnegie Blue) and back to Townley Frocks in 1940, where she launched her own label.

Through the 1940s, McCardell gained a reputation for designing practical womenswear – basic shapes from basic fabrics such as denim, jersey, cotton and gingham, using detail as a means of maintaining a fashion edge. The chief characteristics of her designs were born in their

functionality: deep armholes, rivets and patch pockets. Indeed, such was her immediate influence that many of the key fashions of the 1940s and early 1950s were McCardell-inspired, including her so-called 'monastic' dress (a loose, waistless dress), a one-piece bathing suit, pumps based on the ballet shoe (and made by U.S. ballet shoe company Capezio), play-suits with bloomers, gently pleated dirndl skirts, elasticated tube tops and, especially, what became known as the 'popover', a widely influential kind of wraparound dress.

Designs of McCardell's, such as her black jersey-knit two-piece (which dates from the late 1940s), combined comfort and practicality with style

Stella McCartney

Founder: Stella McCartney
Born: 1971, London, England

Stella McCartney joined Chloé in 1997 in a storm of publicity, partly because she is Beatle Paul's daughter, but also because at only 24 and with a scant CV behind her, the appointment was considered a gamble. But McCartney's debut show, in October 1997, a collection that combined antique detailing such as glass buttons and old lace with the tailoring skills she learned while working on London's Savile Row and for Christian Lacroix, won praise from most critics. A graduate of Central Saint Martins College of Art and Design in London, McCartney's consistent development of Chloé has, at the time of writing, yet to be proven.

Chloé will give McCartney a great opportunity to make her mark, as the French label has tended to follow the imprint of its designer rather than present a consistent signature aesthetic.

The first McCartney designs to make the fashion world sit up and take notice of her featured tailoring with antique lace (1997)

Alexander McQueen

Founder: Alexander McQueen
Born: 1969, London, England

Few young designers can claim to have taken the fashion
world by storm as quickly as boy wonder Alexander
McQueen. Part of the mid-1990s London fashion
renaissance that saw young British designers given some of
the most important jobs in fashion, McQueen was no
exception. He landed a design job at Givenchy in 1996
(taking over from John Galliano) in the same year that he
won the British Designer of the Year award. His first
Givenchy collection was a costume show-stopper, mixing
Roman gladiator breast-plates with cute cupids. Later
collections were tamer (with, for instance, the Japanese-
inspired 1998 collection emitting a Zen-like calm), but his
trademark razor-sharp tailoring was no less impressive.

Alexander McQueen was born in London's East End,
the son of a cab-driver. He began work at 16 as a pattern
cutter for London's Savile Row tailors Anderson & Shepard,
before moving on to Gieves & Hawkes. He then worked for
Koji Tatsuno and Romeo Gigli in Italy before winning a
scholarship to study at Central Saint Martins College of Art

Never one to let practicality obstruct attention-grabbing
design, McQueen created his bumster trousers in 1995

and Design in London. He launched his own business in 1993 and was assisted in his rise by stylist Isabella Blow (now fashion director for the *Sunday Times*), who championed him after seeing his master's thesis collection.

His eponymous line was launched in 1992 and his shows have garnered critical acclaim and dampened media suggestions that his talent would inevitably burn out – the result, ironically, of his an ability to catch the wider media's attention. In his summer 1999 collection he used a model with prosthetic legs (a move which generated wider discussions about fashion's role in society, received notions of beauty, and fashion's reliance on obvious erogenous zones).

Other collections have provoked more outrage. His low-slung 'bumster' trousers resulted in tabloid frenzy, while his 'Highland Rape' collection of slashed tartan dresses, worn by blood-splattered models was, McQueen said, to commemorate England's 18th-century pillage of Scotland. Unfortunately, few saw it that way. Similarly, his summer 1995 show, in which models were bound in sellotape and marked with a tyre-track print, was met with accusations of misogyny. Such criticisms haven't, however, stopped McQueen's ascendancy, nor his willingness to shock.

Alexander
McQueen

Issey Miyake

Founder: Issey Miyake
Born: 1935, Hiroshima, Japan

Issey Miyake has a radical design aesthetic, at once futuristic and historic (often based on the costumes of his native Japan). Bold, with geometric, rigid structures that stand alone from but enhance the body's shape, his work is a mix of Eastern and Western sensibilities.

In 1965, he left the Tama Art University in Tokyo to study fashion at the Ecole de la Chambre Syndicale de la Couture Parisienne. On graduating, he worked for Guy Laroche (on the tailored ready-to-wear lines) and, from 1968, for Givenchy. He left Paris for New York in 1969, joined Geoffrey Beene and then set up on his own. His first show was held in New York in 1971.

The Miyake Design Studio was established in 1970 to research and develop new fabrics and cutting techniques. Successes of the studio have included 'second skin' polyester jersey fabrics, hemp-based materials, Miyake's trademark layered and textured styles and, through the 1990s, intricate pleats. Miyake designed pleated jackets for the Lithuanian Olympic team at the 1992 Barcelona Olympics and his Pleats Please collection is now a diffusion line in its own right.

Trademark intricate pleats and rigid structures from 1989

Moschino

Founder: Franco Moschino
Born: 1950, Abbiategrasso, Italy
Died: 1994, France

Franco Moschino was the arch humorist of fashion, who spoke out against the ridiculousness of that world. He always devoted his energy to issues that he considered more important, notably ecology and animal rights. Many of his designs came close to mocking the women who wore them.

One could perhaps trace this designer's broad viewpoint back to his informal fashion education. Moschino spent his early life doing odd jobs, then began life drawing in Milan at the Accademia di belle Arti and there started designing for fashion houses. On graduating in 1971, Moschino got an illustrating job with Versace, before designing at Cadette in 1978. He launched his own business in 1983.

Some designs have been gimmicky, but others have shown his expert tailoring: winter hats made of teddies stitched together – huddling for warmth, perhaps – windmills or mini-fried eggs as blazer buttons, golden safety pins holding together evening tops (before Versace's Elizabeth Hurley dress), and dinner suits with knife and fork motifs. In recent years, the empire has expanded into jeans, casualwear, lingerie, shoes and perfume.

Moschino's 1996 collection included a suit with a very bold leaf and flower pattern, which looked like camouflage

Thierry Mugler

Founder: Thierry Mugler
Born: 1948, Strasbourg, France

'The Mugler woman is a conqueror who controls her looks and her life. She is free, self-confident and she's having fun... Every woman has a goddess within. I like to bring her out... What I am trying to say with these extravagant clothes is that everything is possible.' So said Thierry Mugler, one of fashion's most innovative and excessive designers and one who takes pride in blurring the boundaries between fashion and theatre.

As well as the usual supermodels, Mugler's catwalk shows have been graced with some of the world's most famous performers, from James Brown to Diana Ross, Julie Newmar to Sharon Stone, and have been 'performed' in sports stadia. And his clothes are equally flamboyant, both his much admired ready-to-wear and his often shocking haute couture. (Mugler also has a reputation for mixing made-to-measure garments in with his ready-to-wear collections.) They are distinct in their emphasis of the female form through exaggeration of waists, hips and shoulders, and rich with extensive references – from fetishism to sci-fi and, perhaps most notably, classic Hollywood musicals of the 1940s and 1950s. But Mugler cannot simply be pigeon-holed as over-the-top. His repertoire, while criticized as vulgar by some fashion watchers, also extends to the most formal of minimalism.

Mugler trained for a year as a dancer with Strasbourg's Opera de Rhine (a training which perhaps accounts for both his love of theatre and appreciation of the human form) before joining the School of Fine Arts in the same city. On graduation at 20 years old, he worked in Paris as a window-dresser and design assistant for the Gudule boutique, before living in Amsterdam and London between 1968 and 1971, freelancing for André Peters in London and for other fashion houses in Milan and Paris. Mugler returned to Paris in 1971 to launch his first collection under the name Café de Paris. Two years later his collection was launched under his own name.

Mugler's autumn/winter 1995 collection characteristically showed his love of drama and 1940s glamour, particularly the dress and cape combination

Mugler

Jean Muir

Founder: Jean Muir
Born: 1933, London, England
Died: 1995, London, England

Jean Muir's rise to her position as one of the most influential designers of the Swinging Sixties was a fairy-tale rise from the shop floor. Her clothing achieved a classic, simple but intricately structured fluidity that was regarded in the fashion world as being without equal. This she achieved through working complicated cutting, tailoring and punching techniques on to her preferred fabrics of jersey or suede. She had no formal fashion training.

Muir joined the London department store Liberty in 1950 to work in the stock room, but was soon out from behind the scenes to sell in the made-to-measure department – where she got her first taste of construction – before moving on to sketching designs for Liberty. By 1956 she had a job with Jaeger (which had been producing its own clothing line since the late 1920s), launching her own line under the name Jane & Jane in 1961. Five years later the Jean Muir fashion name and business was established. During the 1960s her peasant dresses, shawls, two-piece dresses and loose knee-length, flat-collared smocks were influential internationally.

Muir

Prada

Prada

Designer: Miuccia Prada
Born: 1949, Milan, Italy

The original Prada company was established as Fratelli Prada in 1913 in Milan by Mario Prada. But by the 1970s the company had been consistently outshone by the likes of Hermès and Gucci, and was on the verge of bankruptcy. Prada's revival can be attributed to its designer Mario's granddaughter Miuccia Prada. She and her husband Bertelli somewhat reluctantly took control of the business in 1978. Bertelli handles management. Miuccia introduced Prada's signature black nylon accessories.

Alongside Gucci, Prada represented a turnaround of unexpected proportions. For several seasons, Prada heavily influenced fashion's direction both at high and street-fashion levels. Traditional garments were revolutionized and given a sharp, streamlined, simple look. The introduction of technical, futuristic-style sportswear, the Prada Sport line, and a footwear range that was so widely copied that it was, for a time, hard to find anything that wasn't a Prada rip-off, sealed Prada's authority.

Despite perhaps a lack of appreciation for the company's roots, to many young fashion-followers Prada became the ultimate status symbol of the 1990s. Poor copies of Prada's signature black and silver metal triangle badge appeared on street-market imitations. And for Prada, the public's desire to own the real McCoy allowed it to create demand for its often essentially basic products, such as its black nylon rucksacks.

Such was the demand for Prada products at the end of the decade that the estimated value of the company was around $800 million. Clearly, during its style overhaul, the company also turned a corner in its business approach, changing from being a somewhat quaint specialist Milanese business to becoming aggressively acquisitive, buying and selling (at a great profit) up to 9.5% stakes in rival Gucci, as well as acquiring the entire business of admired designer Helmut Lang in 1999. It also bought the Jil Sander label that year, although Sander herself was to depart in January 2000, after only five months. Other lines were also launched to critical and commercial acclaim. As well as Sport, there is Granello and the youth-oriented Miu Miu line, launched in 1992. The company also increased publicity at the end of the 1990s. In addition to its consistently sophisticated press advertising campaigns, Prada Sport's participation in the America's Cup yacht race in 2000, for instance, helped raise its profile further. Bertelli has stated a desire to give the Sport line's red stripe logo the same global brand power as the Nike swoosh.

One of the most recent departures for the old Milanese company was to start producing black nylon accessories in addition to shoes and clothes. These were very much in evidence in the 1999 collection

Paul Poiret

Founder: Paul Poiret
Born: 1879, Paris, France
Died: 1944, Paris, France

Paul Poiret claimed to have freed women from the tyranny of the corset with designs which were more loose and informal. At the start of the 20th century, he produced simple, fitted gowns in contrast to the rib-wrenching styles that dominated the period. Corsets were lowered and the number of underclothes cut back for a more relaxed and easy-to-wear shape. Always inspired by oriental dress, Poiret's designs were also linked with kimono shapes, one of these becoming popular through the patronage of actress Isadora Duncan. Later years saw the introduction of harem pants, turbans and tall feathers worn in both hair and hats.

With such dramatic styles, Poiret used rich, bold, textured fabrics, including silks, lamé, velvets and brocade. He later designed fabrics for the Bianchini-Ferier textiles company, often with artist Raoul Dufy. Not all Poiret designs were successful: his hobble skirt confined the ankles and was much criticized. But he expanded his business into other areas. His Ecole Martine, established just before World War I, employed untrained women to design textiles.

One of his most influential designs was the so-called 'lampshade' dress, using a wired tunic on which the hem stood away from the body. He was similarly ahead of his time in encouraging the wearing of trousers under skirts.

The son of a Paris cloth merchant, Poiret first worked for an umbrella-maker, sketching fashions in his spare time and eventually selling them to Madame Cheruit at the house of Raudnitz Seours. By 1899, he had joined Jacques Doucet (designer of extravagant dresses, tea gowns and tailored suits) and had a big hit with one design, a red cape, assisted by the patronage of actress Réjane. In 1901 he moved to Charles Frederick Worth (most famous for his white tulle evening gowns), opening his own house in 1903, but due to changing fashions the company did not relaunch after World War I.

Dresses such as the sleeveless gold and black 'Samovar' dress of 1919 helped rid the world of the tyranny of the corset

Mary Quant

Founder: Mary Quant
Born: 1934, London, England

A household name in London's Swinging Sixties, Mary Quant began her career as a retailer of other designers' clothes before launching her own ranges. Her clothes were successful because they were simple, affordable and yet defiantly of the times.

Quant was born in London in 1934. She attended London's Goldsmith's College of Art from 1950 to 1953, then worked with London milliner Erik. She left him to open Bazaar, with Archie McNair and Alexander Plunket Green. Green was later to become her husband.

Soon magazines were featuring her skinny rib sweaters, hipster belts and crochet tops. Among her futuristic innovations was a collection of wet-look PVC garments.

In 1963 she began designing for the J. C. Penny chain store and Puritan Fashions in the U.S., although her name-making move came with the launch of the Quant cosmetics line in 1966.

Perhaps her greatest contribution to fashion was the mini-skirt, also made in 1966. Fans typically teamed this with matching sweater and tights to create a uniform look.

Mary Quant gave the world more than make-up and the mini-skirt. She also produced simple, elegant clothes such as the knee-length beige coat with patch pockets (1964)

Paco Rabanne

Founder: Paco Rabanne
Born: 1934, San Sebastian, Spain

Paco Rabanne was born the son of the chief seamstress at Balenciaga's Spanish business. He was educated in France (where the family moved when General Franco took power), studying architecture at the Ecole des Beaux-Arts in Paris from 1952 to 1964. On leaving he immediately applied his architectural knowledge to making innovative buttons for Balenciaga, Nini Ricci and Givenchy, moving on to design distinctive and popular bright plastic jewellery, which he successfully sold to Balenciaga, Givenchy and Dior.

Rabanne began designing clothes in alternative materials, notably plastic, in 1965, and opened his own fashion house in the following year, quickly making a name for himself as a unique, almost bizarre figure in the world of fashion.

It's not usual for fashion designers to get involved in world affairs, let alone predict the end of the world – to the precise day. But then Paco Rabanne isn't your average designer. He has spoken of our entry into the age of Aquarius, announced that he met God at a football match, had out-of-body experiences, visited alien civilizations and claimed that he is the reincarnation of one of the Theban priests who murdered Tutankhamun. And all with the same seriousness he applies to hemlines and fabric innovation. He has been described as a couturier, is a vegetarian, an author and also a shaman and an astrologist. He has also been called the Devil; in 1995 a woman sat outside the designer's shop on rue du Cherche Midi and told potential customers that it was 'the devil's store' and that Rabanne had cast a spell over her daughter. Rabanne was eventually forced to take civil action against the woman.

Rabanne the womenswear designer's key contribution is arguably that of being a fashion visionary. Although he often uses traditional materials, assembled to exacting standards, since his first collection in 1966 – called 'Twelve Unwearable Dresses' – he has also used chain-mail, plastic held together with wire, jersey towelling held together with Sellotape, laser discs, paper, plastic bottles, aluminium panels, ostrich plumes, socks and various other paraphernalia in creating his clothes. Rabanne's creations are often torn apart, or made from ripped shreds of fabric (from silk to mink), with the construction techniques clearly exposed. Widely regarded as a pioneer in his use of alternative materials, perhaps unsurprisingly, he was ranked, along with Anton Courrèges, as a key exponent of Space Age fashion in the mid-1960s, and was much in demand as a costume designer for film.

Ever since 1966, Rabanne has embraced innovation and creativity, especially during the 'Space Age' era

Rabanne

Oscar de la Renta

Founder: Oscar de la Renta
Born: 1932, Dominican Republic

Twice winner of the Coty American Fashion Critic's Award and twice president of the Council of Fashion Designers of America (in the 1970s and again in the 1980s), de la Renta has played a key role in developing U.S. fashion since the 1960s.

At the age of 18 de la Renta went to study painting at Madrid's Academia de San Fernando. Then, in the late 1950s, he designed a dress for the daughter of the U.S. Ambassador to Spain which featured on the cover of *Life* magazine. This turned his attention to fashion. After sketching for several Spanish fashion houses, he won an apprenticeship at Balenciaga, leaving Spain in 1961 to join Lanvin-Castillo in Paris. His training there led, in 1963, to designing for Elizabeth Arden in New York. Two years later he joined the Jane Derby company as a partner. The following year the name was changed to his own, and with Gerald Shaw he took full control of the business in 1974.

Throughout this time de la Renta was gaining a reputation for his opulent, colourful clothes. He still corners the market for show-stopping evening gowns and has ongoing ready-to-wear and couture collections.

One of the most flamboyant de la Renta flamenco dresses of his spring/summer 1995 collection

Yves Saint Laurent

Founder: Yves Saint Laurent
Born: 1936, Oran, Algeria

Few designers have been awarded the same accolades as
Yves Saint Laurent. In 1982 he won the Council of the
Fashion Designers of America's International Fashion
Award. The following year New York's Metropolitan
Museum launched a retrospective of his work, which then
transferred to Moscow. He is regarded as a visionary by
other designers, and his influence is often evident in their
work. Saint Laurent has also made shrewd business moves:
in 1993 his own fashion house YSL merged with Elf-
Sanofui, France's state-owned petro-chemical giant.

Yves Saint Laurent was born to a wealthy family. At 17 he
won the dress section of an International Wool Secretariat
design competition, and was hired by Christian Dior. Four
years later, when Dior died, Saint Laurent became the
company's head of design at 21. The death of Dior was a
turning point for Saint Laurent in more ways than one. At
Dior's funeral he met Pierre Berge, who was to become Saint
Laurent's lover and the business brains behind YSL's
transformation into a leading world-wide brand.

Saint Laurent went on to design six collections for Dior,
each acclaimed and each in greater contrast to what many
had come to associate with the Dior name. Each also
revealed an innovation which would become a fashion staple
– beginning with the trapeze dress (a knee-length, parallel-

sided dress based on the trapezium shape) of his debut collection in 1958. It was street fashion seen through the eyes of a high fashion designer.

In 1961 Saint Laurent was discharged from the army after a short spell of national service, owing to illness, and returned to Paris to find that his position at Dior had been filled by Marc Bohan, director of Dior's British operations since 1958. Saint Laurent left Dior to found YSL, introducing both his more personal vision and the beginnings of a global brand in January 1962. His first collection featured pea jackets with gold buttons and silk and satin smocks. Later collections included thigh-high boots, velvet knickerbockers, safari jackets, trouser suits, peasant costumes and the 1965 Mondrian dresses (inspired by the colour blocks of Dutch artist Piet Mondrian's paintings) – all seminal and widely influential designs.

Over the next 30 years Saint Laurent by turns shocked, stunned and soothed the fashion world, moving from young, easy-to-wear designs to sophisticated womenswear, often adapted from the male wardrobe. These ranged from biker jackets and his trademark transparent blouse with black velvet woman's tuxedo of 1966, through to North African influences and turbans in the 1970s and, in the face of power suits, the elegance of the 1980s. The appointment of Tom Ford as creative director in January 2000 ensured that this innovation was to continue well into the 21st century.

During the decade of the 'power suit', Saint Laurent responded with designs like his pink feathers worn with black stockings (1988) which were defiantly 'frothy' and traditionally feminine

Jil Sander

Founder: Jil Sander
Born: 1943, Wesselburen, Germany

Jil Sander grew up in Hamburg where she studied textile design. After moving to California, she worked as a fashion journalist, freelancing for U.S. magazines such as *McCalls* and German titles such as *Petra* and *Constanze*. She designed clothes as a sideline, began freelance designing in 1968 and opened her first shop the same year.

To call Jil Sander the mistress of discreet understatement is in itself an understatement. Sander designs timeless, classic designerwear for those who don't want to be seen to be wearing designer labels. Although immaculately made and admired for its details – clean-lined, razor-sharp, linen shirts, mesh dresses, cuffed trousers, usually in black, white or grey, in rayon, polyester organza and perforated suedes – Sander's sober clothes are not readily identifiable. Which accounts for the low-key celebrities among her clientele.

What makes Sander clothes noteworthy is their construction. A typical creation uses darts, asymmetric cutting, bunching and angled seams. For which, of course, there is a price. Sander's clothes are notoriously expensive, in keeping with her 'you get what you pay for' philosophy – one that makes a diffusion Jil Sander line unlikely.

Sander's clothes, like the grey polo neck brought out in 1999, are subtle in colouring and cut, but not so understated in price

Schiaparelli

Founder: Elsa Schiaparelli
Born: 1890, Rome, Italy
Died: 1973, Paris, France

Elsa Schiaparelli spent her early life in Boston and then New York, and moved to Paris in 1922. An early design of hers (a black sweater with a trompe l'oeil white bow knitted into it) was spotted in 1927 by a store buyer who guaranteed her enough orders to get her business going.

Her first collection arrived in 1929 and was regarded as far ahead of its time. Her clothes were eccentric, playful and witty. This was in part because she commissioned artists such as Jean Cocteau, the Spanish surrealist painter Salvador Dali, jewellery designer Jean Schlumberger (later designer for Tiffany & Co) and the French illustrator and fabric designer Christian Bérard (who also influenced Dior) to come up with new fabric and accessory ideas, but it was also due to her readiness to reject conservatism while still remaining sophisticated.

At a time when most clothing followed a sober palette, she designed brightly coloured clothes, championing what she named 'shocking pink' in particular. She produced designs that would influence others' collections for years to come, including her broad pagoda sleeve, frilled to the elbow and then widened into flounces, which started to define the New Look. Throughout the 1930s, Schiaparelli produced countless new ideas: among others, she padded shoulders in sweaters, dyed furs, exposed dyed zips on garments, used tweed in eveningwear, fashioned outsize buttons and put a pronounced exoskeleton on the outside of an evening dress. She also made glow-in-the-dark brooches and handbags that played tunes or lit up when opened.

She was also a great milliner, making hats in the shape of lamb cutlets and ice-cream cones. Schiaparelli was a designer trained in philosophy who was heavily influenced by art and surrealism in particular.

After World War II ended, she lectured in fashion in Paris. Her last show was held in 1954.

Schiaparelli's black 'Skeleton' evening dress, modern even by today's standards, was made over 60 years ago, in 1938

Paul Smith

Founder: Paul Smith
Born: 1946, Nottingham, England

Paul Smith's rise to the position of Britain's most successful fashion designer began in 1970, when the then 24-year-old designer opened his first store in his native Nottingham – a small shop that opened only on Fridays and Saturdays but was, at the time, one of the few retailers of designer labels outside London. The store also sold Smith's own early, unbranded shirt, trousers and jacket designs – essentially items that he wanted for himself but was unable to find.

Smith studied at evening classes at Nottingham Polytechnic and soon extended his own range of designs with the assistance of his girlfriend Pauline Denyer, a fashion graduate of London's Royal College of Art. By 1974 the shop became a full-time business for him. Two years later he was appointed a consultant both to an Italian shirt manufacturer and to the International Wool Secretariat, positions which persuaded him to show his first collection in Paris. His first London shop opened in 1979. He went on to open stores in New York in 1987 and Paris in 1993.

By the end of the 1990s Smith's self-financed business was operating with a turnover of over £170 million and his contribution to menswear design has been widely applauded. His business spans menswear, womenswear (launched in 1994), underwear, children's clothes, Paul Smith London, PS by Paul Smith, bespoke tailoring, other lines covering jeans, spectacles, toiletries, shoes, bags, watches and R. Newbold, the British workwear company established in the 1880s, who Smith saved from closure by acquisition in 1991.

While noted for being instrumental in the revival of boxer shorts and the Filofax in the early 1980s, Smith has come to be more widely recognized for his individual, yet essentially traditional style. Using Italian, French and British fabrics, most of his designs show what has come to be regarded as a typically English sense of the eccentric and offbeat, offering 'classics with a twist' in unexpected fabrics. Smith's other key signature style has been the introduction to menswear of bold, often humorous prints (particularly on shirts) and an emphasis on quirky accessories, many of which Smith collects himself on his wide travels. His irreverent take on classic styles is particularly popular in Japan where he is considered to be the most successful European designer. By the end of the 1990s, Smith had a chain of over 200 shops in Japan and held pop-star celebrity status there.

In 1991 Paul Smith received the prestigious Royal British Designer for Industry award. He was made a CBE for his services to the fashion industry in 1994. A 25-year retrospective of his work, 'Paul Smith: True Brit', ran at London's Design Museum in 1995.

Paul Smith eccentricity 2000. The designer is famous throughout the world for his shirts with their wacky prints

Richard Tyler

Founder: Richard Tyler
Born: 1946, Sunshine, Australia

One of the few Australian international fashion designers, Richard Tyler left school at 16 and learnt precision tailoring under a tailor trained on London's Savile Row. As a result, most of Tyler's clothes, even those for women, are based around masculine shapes. He began his career by opening a shop in Melbourne called Zippity-doo-dah in the 1960s and designing clothes that were then made by his dressmaker mother. By the 1970s he had established a reputation for creating flamboyant, sexy, but perfectly tailored clothes for rock stars. This reputation was enhanced by his move to Los Angeles where, in 1988, he opened a menswear store. His first women's collection followed the next year.

In 1993, Tyler was appointed head of design for Anne Klein (the U.S. sportswear business). He left at the end of 1994. In 1996, following on from both Guy Paulin and Gianni Versace in earlier years, he was made design director of Byblos, the Italian fashion house specializing in young, often African and Asian-inspired clothing, founded in 1973.

Straight lines and ties. Richard Tyler makes dramatic, sexy clothes for dramatic, sexy people

Tyler

Ungaro

Founder: Emanuel Ungaro
Born: 1933, Aix-en-Provence, France

Emanuel Ungaro was born into an Italian immigrant family. He trained as a tailor with the family business before moving to Paris in 1955, aged 22. There, he took on an apprenticeship with Balenciaga, where he stayed for six years before moving on in 1961 to work under Anton Courrèges for two seasons. Four years later, in 1965, Ungaro launched his own fashion house, making 20 outfits for his first collection. In this he caught the space-age themes of Courrèges and Cardin – all futuristic, sharp-edged tailoring, transparent dresses, thigh-high boots and metal garments – a look that was to soften considerably over the following years into his hallmark of a rich, bold, feminine style.

Ungaro achieved a reputation and a distinct look by breaking fashion rules, compiling in his collection a mishmash of stripes with polka dots and florals with animal prints. This clashing signature approach, made more distinctive for being worn on structured jackets paired with lacy dresses and chiffon skirts, and by his designer's eye for balance, has made Ungaro a widely appreciated name not only in haute couture but also in ready-to-wear, for the

By 1999, Ungaro's initially sharp-edged style had been replaced by softer designs featuring structured jackets with chiffon skirts

collection which he designs under the Parallèle name.

Ungaro's collections have seen evening dresses trimmed with feathers, pearl-brocaded satin dresses, tulle dresses with ruffs, heart-shaped bustiers and a full palette of soft pastels. The collections were sufficiently attractive for the label to be acquired by Salvatore Ferragamo in 1996.

Valentino

Founder: Valentino Garavani
Born: 1932, Voghera, near Milan, Italy

Showing an interest in fashion from an early age, Valentino Garavani studied at Milan's Accademia dell'Arte and then moved to Paris at seventeen to study at the Ecole de la Chambre Syndicale de la Haute Couture. He stayed in Paris to take apprenticeships with fashion houses Jean Desses (for five years) and Guy Laroche (for two) before returning to

Italy in 1959 to launch his own couture business on Rome's Via Condotti – a move made possible largely due to the financial support of his family.

Valentino showed his first international couture collection in Florence in 1962 to an ecstatic response from critics and buyers alike. But it wasn't until the end of the 1960s, when he met Giancarlo Giammetti, an architectural student who abandoned his studies to become Valentino's business partner, that Valentino took his first steps towards the founding of a vast fashion empire.

It was Valentino's so-called White Collection of 1967 – which saw the introduction of his 'V' logo – that sealed his success and made him a household name in his homeland. The collection expressed a new purity and simplicity at a time when fashion was dedicated to colour and pop culture. As well as introducing Valentino's signature sense of details – notably big bows and embroidered stockings – it included a white lace mini-dress that was dedicated to Jackie Kennedy and which she was to wear at her marriage to Aristotle Onassis.

The marriage was, naturally, on countless magazine covers around the globe and it helped to establish Valentino's reputation among the socialite set as a designer of must-have clothes. Within two years he had launched ready-to-wear collections for men and women, and opened two stores, in Rome and Milan.

Further stores opened around the world, notably in Japan and the U.S., until he had well over sixty outlets. Shirts, jeans, accessories, ties, furniture, wallpaper and fabric were all to bear the celebrated 'V', with Valentino also launching a younger diffusion line called Oliver, named after his dog.

Valentino introduced his first perfume in 1978 – with typical flamboyance – at a gala at the Theatre des Champs Elysées in Paris, where Mikhail Baryshnikov danced. In 1989 Valentino opened an art exhibition space in Rome called the Accademia Valentino. The same year saw the launch, in conjunction with his friend Elizabeth Taylor, of LIFE, an association supporting AIDS sufferers.

Almost 30 years after Valentino's 'White Collection', white was still a significant element in his 1995 show, which featured a white lace mini-dress

Versace

Founder: Gianni Versace
Born: 1946, Reggio Calabria, Italy
Died: 1997, Miami, U.S.A.

The son of a couturier, Gianni Versace was always destined to work in fashion. He worked for his mother from the age of 18, then studied architecture in Milan before starting his fashion career aged 25. His break came when he obtained work designing for Lucca's Florentine Flowers clothing factory. He was soon designing knitwear for Italian ready-to-wear company Genny, and leatherwear for Complice (which Versace had some part in launching in 1974 and which went on to be designed by Dolce & Gabbana).

Versace showed his own collection in 1978. It featured finely-tailored, body-conscious and defiantly sexy outfits with dresses low-cut and skirts slit high. In 1979, he launched his menswear collection. Gianni Versace's clothes have a reputation for veering between the most luxurious of refined eveningwear to the gaudiest, most golden rock-star paraphernalia around. Madonna, Prince, Jon Bon Jovi, Tina Turner, Phil Collins and Elton John are all fans.

Versace was a master at mixing eye-popping prints (especially his signature Romanesque motifs, Greek Medusa and animal prints), bright colours, slinky shapes, historical referencing and rich fabrics to make a show-stopping confection of fashion and art – a combination the designer believed to be inseparable. The power of his clothes to attract attention was proven by the tight evening dress, held together by golden safety pins, that appeared on every front page and made actress and model Elizabeth Hurley's name. Versace also designed for Diana, Princess of Wales, and Princess Caroline of Monaco.

Perhaps unsurprisingly, from 1982 Versace's design flamboyance extended to designing for opera and theatre. Less predictably, he was also able to extend his original aesthetic to create an empire which covers fragrances, homewares, jewellery and china. The Versace business – which has been valued at well in excess of 1,700 billion lire and operates over 135 shops worldwide – also produces diffusion and spin-off lines, among them Istante and Versus.

Some Versace designs have entered the fashion pantheon as classics, most notably his metallic mesh dresses. Versace epitomized the high life, the dress code for the fabulously wealthy and indiscreet. When he was shot dead in Miami, the reputation remained. Gianni's siblings, Donatella and Santo Versace, took over responsibility for design and business respectively after his death.

Gianni Versace will be remembered as being one of the most important fashion designers of the 1980s and 1990s.

Never has a garment propelled anyone into the limelight as effectively as the Versace dress worn by Liz Hurley for the premiere of *Four Weddings and a Funeral* in 1994

Versace

Roger Vivier

Founder: Roger Vivier
Born: 1913, Paris, France
Died: 1998, Toulouse, France

Roger Vivier studied sculpture at the Ecole des Beaux-Arts in Paris and turned to shoe design when it was suggested he should design a range for a shoe factory. This led to several other commissions and, in 1937, to the opening of his own fashion house. Commissions followed from all over the world.

Vivier signed a design contract with Delman in 1938 which was set to be a long-term association, but World War II intervened. After a year's service, Vivier returned to Delman until 1941. After a break in which he opened a New York shop with Parisian milliner Suzanne Remi in 1942, he returned to Delman in 1947. From 1947 he worked freelance for Dior in Paris until the French couturier opened a shoe department in his store in 1953 and Vivier was officially appointed designer. Notable commissions included garnet-studded kidskin for the heels of Queen Elizabeth II's 1953 Coronation shoes, and pairs designed specifically for Catherine Deneuve, The Beatles and Josephine Baker.

Vivier's work for Christian Dior from the early 1950s sealed his reputation as one of the century's most influential shoe designers. His designs included

contemporary evening versions of 18th-century mules, court shoes made using the technology and materials of the aeronautical world, 1957's particularly popular stacked, chisel-toed, leather-heeled shoes, and many other styles displaying a particular use of opulent materials. Vivier's signature style is in his innovative heel designs, usually named after the shape they mimic, such as the 'needle' or 'escargot' (snail).

Pink satin court shoe with studded band. By the time this was available, in 1965, Vivier was well established as shoemaker to the stars

Louis Vuitton

Founder: Louis Vuitton
Born: 1821, Anchay, France
Died: 1892, Asnières, France

Louis Vuitton was founded in 1854 by Louis Vuitton, the son of a carpenter. In 1834 he travelled to Paris to work as a luggage-maker, launching his luggage company on the rue Neuve des Capucines 20 years later. From the start, he sought to distinguish his leather goods from the competition by using the best materials and craftsmanship, a reputation for which the brand was quickly known. These were luxury products for luxury people – often one-offs (personalized manufacture became a Vuitton philosophy), such as a 1930s crocodile skin and tortoiseshell toiletries case, and bags in ostrich, lizard and other luxury leathers. Cleverly, in the late 1800s, Vuitton also anticipated new forms of travel and designed easily-stowed, flat-topped trunks. He was aware also of the need to make his own products outdated – canvas coverings were redesigned every few years to inspire the fashion-conscious to buy new sets.

The famous LV monogram and patented lock were invented by Vuitton's son Georges in 1896 (his son Gaston also joined the firm). Several pieces became classics. These included the Noé, designed in 1932 for a champagne house (it held five bottles) and the Alma bag, designed in 1920 for Coco Chanel. The first London store opened in 1885 and by the 1990s Vuitton had over 200 stores worldwide.

Vivienne Westwood

Founder: Vivienne Westwood
Born: 1941, Glossop, England

Vivienne Westwood spent a short time at Harrow Art School before leaving to train as a teacher. Her first forays into fashion came after meeting Malcolm McLaren, with whom she opened a fashion shop which eventually became 'Sex' (though the name changed regularly) in London's King's Road in the late 1960s. During the 1970s, tying in her designs with his management of a young, aggressive and front-page story-making band called the Sex Pistols, Westwood was given a ready launch platform for her fashion, notably experimenting at the time with leather and fetish clothing. She showed her first full collection, the 'Buffalo Collection', with its Peruvian peasant-inspired sheepskin capes and reinforced bras worn over sweaters, in Paris in 1981.

Arguably one of the most important and widely influential fashion designers of the century, Vivienne Westwood's designs have encompassed the aggressive and the stereotypically feminine, heavily referenced the past and set up fashions for the future, been born of the street (and also inspired it), been inspired by traditional clothing – and yet always suggest sex. The clothes have been criticized as unwearable and yet led to the dress code of at least two

major cultural movements of recent decades: punk in the 1970s and new romanticism in the 1980s.

Her collections have included bustles, hour-glass corsets, fake fur knickers, slogan T-shirts, pirate costumes, S&M-inspired clothing, 9-inch platforms (from which model Naomi Campbell famously fell on the catwalk), mink G-strings, 'micro-crinoline' (or 'mini-crinnie') skirts and clashing tartans.

Much of Westwood's design is historically-based, displays fine tailoring and frequently offers a commentary on wider social shifts, though this is not always easy to see without Westwood's explanation. Most fashion combinations have been given the Westwood consideration, and most of her designs have had an impact on fashion, usually at street level. Later collections, such as 'Savages' and 'Hobos', prefigured grunge, with other details of her designs, such as exposed seams, becoming the basis of the deconstructionist fashion movement that was emerging. Her buckled and strapped 'Bondage' collection of 1976 still has resonance 25 years later, for instance. In the following decade, Westwood's business came to include fragrances, shops, a menswear collection, Vivienne Westwood Red and the diffusion line Anglomania.

Westwood's achievements are all the more remarkable for her being, unlike her peers, a self-taught designer.

Perhaps Westwood's most famous creation since the punk movement, her cupid-print bustier made several appearances on the catwalk after the mid-1980s and before this 1995 version

Yohji Yamamoto

Founder: Yohji Yamamoto
Born: 1943, Toyko, Japan

Yamamoto attended the Keio University until 1966 and then studied at the Bunka Fashion College in Tokyo, Japan. In 1970 he began designing on a freelance basis, and his own 'Y' womenswear line followed in 1972. He showed his first collection in Tokyo in 1977, showing in Paris in 1981. The reaction to the bland and sophisticated look of his clothes was mixed. In 1982 Yamamoto showed in New York and generated a greater buzz. But his real launch into fashion came with the summer collection of 1983, which wrapped the body in swathes of loose fabric, harking back to the his Japanese roots. His aesthetic seemed visionary in contrast to the power-dressing then prevalent.

Yamamoto's stark, sober clothes rarely do themselves justice on a hanger – even when the designer makes his occasional moves away from black, navy and white and takes up orange, powder blue and green. When worn, however, their intricate tailoring and signature details, such as the asymmetric cut or kimono sleeves of his men's suits or shirts, allow the wearer to understand why Yamamoto is one of the most revered, if low-key, of the world's designers. He is the only Japanese designer to be awarded the prestigious French Chevalier de l'Ordre des Arts et Lettres.

Yamamoto does not design clothes that follow flash-in-the-pan seasonal trends and rarely does he stray into the purely conceptual approach of fellow Japanese designer Rei Kawakubo of Comme des Garçons. He has matched Geisha dresses with fedora hats, and used deliberately frayed fabrics on his designs, yet still the results could be worn year after year. His emphasis has always been on designing garments that are timeless: hence his basic, strong silhouette, often finding its roots in traditional workwear or peasant dress, and his use of hardy fabrics. Yamamoto himself puts this down to being part of the first generation that grew up wearing second-hand clothes, and rejecting fashion as a system that is an economic trap because it produces garments that are soon obsolete. He now owns a multi-million pound business, replete with the standard fragrance.

Low-key Yamamoto. His kimono-sleeved peasant dress of 1993 shows how he combines Western and Eastern influences

Glossary

APPLIQUÉ: a process involving stitching one, often floral, piece of fabric on to another for ornamental purposes. Popular in the 1950s and 1970s

BATEAU NECKLINE: a boat-shaped neckline

BERMUDA SHORTS: knee-length shorts originating in 1930s/1940s Bermuda, where women were not allowed to show their legs

BIAS-CUTTING: a cut across the grain of a fabric, to allow it to drape smoothly

BLOOMERS: a loose-fitting garment, the trouser-legs of which gather between knee and ankle. First designed to be worn under a skirt

BOXY JACKETS: jackets producing a broad outline in the wearer, often due to padding in the shoulders

BROCADE: fabric woven on a jacquard loom, characterized by its raised pattern

BROGUE: a shoe, often brown, which is decorated with a pattern of holes. Traditionally worn in Scotland and Ireland

BUBBLE SKIRT: bubble-shaped skirt first designed by Cardin in the late 1950s

BUSTIER: undergarment with origins in the 19th century, combining the functions of a brassière and a corset

CAPRI PANTS: loose trousers that taper from hip to halfway down the calf

COOLIE HAT: a cone-shaped hat of bamboo or straw, typically worn by labourers in south-east Asia

COLOURIST: a designer adept at bringing together differently coloured fabrics

COUTURE or HAUTE COUTURE: clothing made as a one-off or in limited numbers

CRINOLINE: a frame made of hoops over which the skirt of a dress is draped to make the skirt fuller. First popular in the 1840s

CUMMERBUND: a satin/silk waist sash derived from the traditional dress of South American and Indian men, but also worn by Western men as part of their dinner dress

DÉCOLLETAGE: the area of a woman's body between the neck and the top of the bust, often exposed by a dress in a flattering manner

DIFFUSION: a line produced by a designer as a 'spin-off', usually more accessible than the main collection in terms of design and price

DIRNDL SKIRT: full skirt gathered at the waistband to create pleats

DOLMAN: a floor-length wrap, usually fringed or trimmed with lace and with loose sleeves

DOLMAN SLEEVES: sleeves with armholes which extend to a garment's waistline

EMPIRE LINE: a low-cut dress gathered under the bust

FEDORA HAT: a brimmed felt hat with centre-creased crown

FLY-AWAY BACK: where a garment is cut with extra fabric, so that it stands out, usually around the middle or lower back of the wearer

FOULARD: a thin, soft fabric

FROCKCOAT: an adaptation of the long-sleeved, knee-length military coat, originating in the 19th century

GRUNGE: a dressed-down or scruffy style of dress, typified by loose and worn clothing

HACKING JACKET: fitted tweed jacket, traditionally worn for horseriding

HALTER NECK: a neckline on a top or dress which fastens behind the neck, leaving the back and shoulders exposed

HAREM PANTS: divided skirt or trousers gathered at the ankle. Worn as evening-wear at the beginning of the 20th century

HIPSTERS: skirts or trousers which fit around the hips rather than the waist. Originally popular in the 1960s, they had something of a revival in the 1990s

HOBBLE SKIRT: a skirt designed by Poiret which narrowed dramatically at a point between the knee and the ankle, thus shortening (or hobbling) the steps of the wearer

HOT PANTS: shorts which are very short and tight, and often come in bright colours

JELLY SHOES: plastic shoes traditionally worn by children, but adapted in the 1880s for adults

JODPHURS: often tightly fitting trousers, traditionally worn for horseriding and originating from a place of the same name in India

JUMPSUIT: 'all in one', zipped suit, traditionally worn by parachutists, but adopted by Fiorucci

LAMÉ: fabric woven from metallic threads, typically gold or silver

LIFESTYLE BRANDING: that which attempts to persuade a customer that they are buying not merely an article of clothing but a whole new way of life

LYCRA: Du Pont-created fabric with strong stretch and recovery properties

MAXI COAT: an ankle or floor-length coat popular in the 1960s

MESH DRESS: a dress made of closely woven netting which may or may not be transparent

MINI CRINNIE: a short version of the crinoline

MOB CAP: a large cap worn indoors during the 19th century and brought back in the 60s by Biba

MOD: a U.K. youth movement of the late 1950s and early 1960s. Mods were characterized by their short hair and neat, Italian-inspired dress. They also wore 'parka' jackets and rode motor scooters

MULE: a woman's shoe with just one strap which passes over the top of the foot behind the toes

NEW LOOK: a term first applied by U.S. fashion editor Carmel Snow to Dior's 1947 collection. Typified by large, billowing skirts teamed with tight, fitted bodices

NEW ROMANTIC: a particular 1980s fancy-dress style of clothing, typically inspired by pirates, highwaymen and 18th-century dandies

ORGANDY: chemically stiffened light, sheer cotton fabric

OXFORD: a low-cut, laced shoe

PAGODA SLEEVE: a style popular for women's dress in the mid-19th century, where each sleeve consisted of several tiers of fabric. Each tier would often be decorated with ribbons

PARKA: a long, loose, casual jacket, usually hooded, and particularly popular with Mods in the 1950s and 1960s

PATCH POCKETS: pockets sewn on to the outside of a garment. Usually large and square in shape

PEA-JACKET/COAT: a warm, double-breasted, woollen coat worn in the 19th century especially by sailors and fishermen

PLATFORM SOLES: thick, raised soles

POPOVER: a wraparound dress designed by U.S. designer Claire McCardell in 1942, which became a classic in that country

PRINCESS LINE: a waistless, clean-lined, narrow-fitting style of dress

PUMPS: flat, comfortable shoes. Originally worn by servants, the term has come to refer to almost any informal, functional shoe

PUNK: dress style originating in 1970s London, characterized by brightly coloured, spiky or cropped hair, defaced or distressed clothing and safety pins, chains and metal studs

PVC: polyvinyl fabric – shiny, plastic-looking fabric often used for outerwear as an alternative to leather

READY-TO-WEAR: mass-produced, ready-made clothing, as opposed to couture

RIVET: a small metal stud often used on jeans to hold together pieces of fabric which would otherwise be liable to come apart or fray

SACK DRESSES: dating from the 1950s, these are loose dresses which taper to below the knee

SHEATH DRESS: a tight-fitting, straight, ankle-length, sleeved dress

SHIFT DRESS: simple smock-style dress, typically opening at the front

SKINNY RIB SWEATERS: tight-fitting jumpers popular in the 1960s

SLING-BACK SANDALS: characterized by a strap above the wearer's heel, these shoes first appeared in the 1920s

STAND-AWAY COLLAR: a shirt collar cut so that the two edges of the collars which usually face each other lie at angles sloping away from each other instead

STREET STYLE: clothing worn by youth of late 20th century, often work- or sportswear-inspired

SWEETHEART NECKLINE: dress or blouse neckline cut to resemble a heart shape

TEA GOWN: a long-sleeved, high-waisted gown designed, in the mid-19th century, to allow for the loosening of a corset underneath it

TENCEL: trademarked hardwearing synthetic fabric

TOILE: garment pattern made from muslin for the purpose of making copies

TUBE TOPS: garments which appear to be cut from a single tube of fabric, usually with only one seam

TUBULAR TROUSERS: usually straight trousers, the legs of which most often have one seam, as opposed to two

TULLE: a fine, mesh fabric used in dress-making, particularly in bridalwear.

TURTLENECK: a jumper with a high, tight neckline

TWIN SET: a matching cardigan and sweater combination originally worn by women in the 1930s, but popular again today

ULTRASUEDE: trademarked synthetic polyester/ polyurethane crease-resistant fabric

WEDGE HEEL: wedge-shaped sole, blurring sole and heel into one unit

COLLINS GEM
BABIES' names
a ? z
a mine of information

COLLINS GEM
BEER
a mine of information

COLLINS GEM
BIRDS
a mine of information

COLLINS GEM
CALORIE
Counter
a mine of information

COLLINS GEM
FACT FILE
a mine of information

COLLINS GEM
FENG SHUI
a mine of information

COLLINS GEM
FLAGS
a mine of information

COLLINS GEM
Healthy
EATING
a mine of information

COLLINS GEM
QUOTATIONS
a mine of information

COLLINS GEM
SAS
Self-Defence
a mine of information

COLLINS GEM
SAS
Survival Guide
a mine of information

COLLINS GEM
SEASHORE
a mine of information

COLLINS GEM
TREES
a mine of information

COLLINS GEM
Understanding
DREAMS
a mine of information

COLLINS GEM
WILD
flowers
a mine of information

COLLINS GEM
WINE
Dictionary
a mine of information